HIDDEN SECRETS OF MASONRY

Dr. Cathy Burns

SHARING
212-M E. 7th St.
Mt. Carmel, PA 17851-2211

Contents

1. IS FREEMASONRY FREE?

Most people who join Masonic organizations have no idea what Masonry **ACTUALLY** teaches. Many join for social reasons while others join for the benefits and prestige it offers. When they enter the Masonic Lodge they are faced with many symbols—all with **HIDDEN** meanings. The purpose of this book is to reveal some of what takes place in the Lodge as well as the **SECRET** meanings behind several of the symbols represented there.

Even Masonic leaders are well aware that the **MAJORITY** of people who join the Masons **DO NOT** really know what Masonry teaches. W. L. Wilmshurst, a highly recognized Masonic writer, states:

> A candidate proposing to enter Freemasonry has **SELDOM** formed **ANY** definite idea of the nature of what he is engaging in. **EVEN AFTER HIS ADMISSION HE USUALLY** remains quite **AT A LOSS** to explain satisfactorily what Masonry is and **FOR WHAT PURPOSE** his Order exists [emphasis mine throughout].[1]

Delmar Darrah, a 33rd degree Mason, explains: "The average man enters Freemasonry with **LITTLE** or **NO KNOWLEDGE** of the fraternity, its manner of organization, or its system of doing business,"[2] but

> ...the Mason **WHO CAN AFFORD IT,** takes all the degrees **WHICH HIS FINANCES** will permit, and seeks to broaden as far as possible his knowledge of those great fundamental truths which distinguish Freemasonry....[3]

There are more than 1,000 degrees that can be awarded from various allied Masonic fraternities.[4] A few of these organizations are: Mystic Shrine; Eastern Star; Acacia; Knights Templar; Daughters of the Nile; Job's Daughters; Rainbow for Girls; Order of DeMolay for Boys; American Lodge of Research; National Sojourners; Ladies' Oriental Shrine of North America; Ancient and Accepted Scottish Rite of Freemasonry; York Rite; Order of the Golden Key; Order of the Constellation of Junior Stars; Order of the Builders; Ancient Toltec Rite; Masonic Relief Association of the U.S.A. and Canada; Royal Order of Jesters; Low Twelve Clubs; Order of Desoms; Order of Amaranth; and Holy Royal Arch Knight Templar Priests.

Albert Pike, probably **THE MOST REVERED OF ALL** Masonic authors, declares that:

Nothing excites men's curiosity so much as Mystery, **CONCEALING** things which they desire to know: and nothing so much increases curiosity as **OBSTACLES** that interpose to prevent them from indulging in the gratification of their desires. Of this the Legislators and Hierophants took advantage, to attract the people to their sanctuaries, and to induce them to seek to obtain lessons from which **THEY WOULD PERHAPS HAVE TURNED AWAY WITH INDIFFERENCE,** if they had been pressed upon them.[5]

Here we can see that **CURIOSITY OF THE UNKNOWN** drove many to the Mysteries to try to **DISCOVER SECRETS.** Pike plainly admits that if these same Mysteries were presented **WITHOUT** the veil of **SECRECY,** these same people "would perhaps have **TURNED AWAY WITH INDIFFERENCE....**"[6] So, to save **CURIOUS** Masons (or those wishing to join Masonry) money, let's see what Masonry teaches from the mouths of Masons **THEMSELVES.**

We are told that Masons believe in charity and good works, but Masonic writer, Ralph Anderson, a 32nd degree Mason, proclaims: "If the **SOLE** value is ethical [**MORAL**]...then Masonry has failed...."[7] Arthur Waite, another Masonic writer, tells us that Masonry "is **ON THE SURFACE** a 'system of morality, **VEILED** in allegory and illustrated by symbols.'"[8] These symbols are used in order to **HIDE** a "deeper truth" which will be revealed **LITTLE BY LITTLE** as the Mason progresses through the degrees. Anderson further expounds on the **HIDDEN SYMBOLISM** of Masonry:

> Masonry may be defined as a system of symbols, a collection of allegories and a pictorial form which **VEILS AND HIDES** a truth so general and universal that man cannot live without it. An allegory is a story which is susceptible of **TWO** meanings—an **OUTER ONE** which captivates the fancy and engrosses the attention, and an **INNER ONE** which conveys to the initiate some basic, cosmic and human truth by which a man must live. A symbol is an **OUTER AND VISIBLE** form which **HIDES OR VEILS AN INNER SPIRITUAL** reality. The Masonic Temple work abounds with such symbols, and through them is **REVEALED** to the

intelligent Mason the story of his own progress and also the **EVOLUTIONARY** history of the race of men.[9]

Waite reports:

> ...the newly received Brother has come into a world of **EMBLEMS** or **SYMBOLISM** and **WHATSOEVER** takes place therein has a meaning **BEHIND IT,** being one which is **NOT ALWAYS INDICATED ON THE SURFACE.**[10]

In fact, Masonry **INTENTIONALLY MISLEADS** those Masons who have recently joined. Pike claims: "The symbols and ceremonies of Masonry have **MORE THAN ONE MEANING.** They rather **CONCEAL** than disclose the Truth."[11]

> If you have been disappointed in the first three degrees, *as you have received them*...remember that...symbols were used, not to *reveal* but to *conceal*... [emphasis in the original].[12]

CONFIDENTIAL

"So Masonry jealously **CONCEALS ITS SECRETS, AND INTENTIONALLY LEADS** conceited interpreters **ASTRAY.**"[13] In yet another place Pike confesses:

> The Blue Degrees [the first three degrees of Masonry] are but the outer court or portico of the Temple. **PART** of the symbols are displayed there to the Initiate, but he is **INTENTIONALLY MISLED BY FALSE INTERPRETATIONS. IT IS NOT INTENDED** that he shall understand them; but **IT IS INTENDED** that **HE SHALL IMAGINE HE UNDERSTANDS** them. Their **TRUE EXPLICATION** is reserved for the Adepts [those who have advanced to the highest degrees in Masonry].... It is well enough for the mass of those called Masons, to **IMAGINE** that all is contained in the Blue Degrees; and whoso attempts to **UNDECEIVE** them will **LABOR IN VAIN....**[14]

Finally, Pike adds:

> Masonry, like all the Religions, all the Mysteries, Hermeticism and Alchemy, **CONCEALS** its secrets from **ALL EXCEPT** the

Adepts and Sages, or the Elect, and **USES FALSE EXPLANA-TIONS AND MISINTERPRETATIONS** of its symbols to **MISLEAD** those who deserve only to be misled; to **CONCEAL** the Truth, which it calls Light, from them, and to draw them away from it.[15]

We are told that people from all faiths may join Masonry.

There is nothing in the requirements of Masonry to prevent a Catholic, a Mohammedan, a Jew, a Buddhist, a Protestant, a Mormon, or a member of any other religion from becoming a member.[16]

Waite declares:

Masonry numbers now all classes of **SPIRITUALISTS,** disciples of Swedenborg, representatives of modern school of **OCCULT** thought and even convinced mystics, not to speak of every shade of opinion in churches and sects.

We must remember, however, that Masonry is itself a religion! Although many Masons deny this, Albert Mackey, one of the most revered Masonic authors, writes about "the **RELIGION** of Free-masonry."[17] He tells us:

Look at its [Masonry's] ancient landmarks, its sublime ceremonies, its profound symbols and allegories—all inculcating **RELIGIOUS DOCTRINE,** commanding **RELIGIOUS OB-SERVANCE,** and teaching **RELIGIOUS** truth, and who can deny that it is eminently a **RELIGIOUS INSTITUTION?...**

Masonry, then, is indeed a **RELIGIOUS INSTITUTION;** and on this ground mainly, if not alone, should the religious Mason defend it.[18]

Anderson calls Masonry "a *spiritual* quest [emphasis in the original]."[19] Pike proclaimed: "Every Masonic Lodge is a **TEMPLE OF RELIGION,** and its teachings are **INSTRUCTION IN RELIGION.**"[20] Waite declares "true Masonry remains a Church of God"[21] and Pike reminds us that "Masonry is a *worship* [emphasis in the original]."[22] After all, Masons go to a Masonic **TEMPLE,** they **WORSHIP** at an **ALTAR,** they **KNEEL** before a **SUPREME**

BEING, and they **SWEAR** upon the **"VOLUME OF SACRED LAW,"** whether it be a Bible, the Koran, the Vedas, or any other "scripture" that is acceptable to the majority of the people within the Lodge.[23]

Masonic Lodges in America display the Bible, but don't be deceived by this appearance. Waite explains that the "Bible in the Lodge of an **ENTERED APPRENTICE** [the name of the first degree] is not of religious acceptance as understood by Adepts...."[24] In other words, even the Bible is **ONLY A SYMBOL** of **SOMETHING ELSE,** but the person who is just entering Masonry is **UNAWARE** of this fact! "Our symbols are **MEANINGLESS UNTIL** they are **TRANSLATED,"** confirms Masonic writer Charles Green.[25] It is plain to see that the symbols a Mason encounters in the Lodge do have a **HIDDEN MEANING.** Some of these **HIDDEN MEANINGS** will be disclosed later in this book.

Since Christianity is a religion as well as Masonry, is there any conflict between the two? Darrah quickly assures us:

> There never has been **ANY CONFLICT** between the church and Freemasonry, nor is there a **SINGLE PRINCIPLE** inculcated by the various Christian societies of the world for which Freemasonry does not contend.[26]

However, when one studies Masonic literature, it is **QUITE EVIDENT** that there are **DEFINITE** conflicts between Christianity and Freemasonry.

When a person enters Masonry, he joins what is called a Blue Lodge. Members of this Lodge may earn the first three degrees (called Craft Degrees) which are: **1)** Entered Apprentice; **2)** Fellow-Craft; and **3)** Master Mason. After these three degrees have been earned (**AND PAID FOR!),** one may take further degrees in the Scottish or the York Rite. The highest one may advance in the Scottish Rite is to the 33rd degree, although most Masons never advance pass the third degree. The York Rite awards ten degrees in addition to the three Craft Degrees. The last degree in the York Rite is equivalent to the 33rd degree of the Scottish Rite.[27] Oaths are taken by the candidate and horrible penalties are pronounced upon him should he betray the **SECRETS** of Masonry. For example, the oath to be taken for the first degree is:

> ...binding myself under no less penalty than that of having my throat cut from ear to ear, my tongue torn out by its roots, and buried

in the sands of the sea a cable's length from shore, where the tide ebbs and flows twice in twenty-four hours, should I ever willingly, knowingly, or unlawfully violate this, my Entered Apprentice Oath, so help me God and keep me steadfast.[28]

James 5:12 informs us that "above all things, brethren, **SWEAR NOT,** neither by heaven, neither by earth, neither by **ANY OTHER OATH...**" but the first thing that the person entering Masonry does is to take an **OATH** which is in **VIOLATION** of God's Word. This is the first **AREA OF CONFLICT** between Christianity and Masonry.

Each degree is filled with **SYMBOLISM** and drama. Wilmshurst reports that the first degree (Entered Apprentice) is a "portrayal of the entrance of all men into, first, physical life, and second, into spiritual life...."[29] This degree corresponds to the sacrament of Baptism,[30] he contends, and "we emulate what is written of the joy that exists among the angels of heaven over every sinner who repents and turns toward the light!"[31] Yes, Masons actually claim that turning to Masonry is **EQUIVALENT** to a sinner repenting and being baptized!

Waite believes that in this first degree the candidate has "been born anew"[32] and that he "is restored to light...and...he is told subsequently that **HE IS THE CORNERSTONE** of a new foundation from which **HE MUST BUILD HIMSELF....**"[33] Here we see that the person who receives the first degree of Masonry is considered to be a "cornerstone of a new foundation" and that "he must build himself." However, the Bible signifies that **JESUS** is the cornerstone, **NOT WE OURSELVES!** Of course, the Bible states that Christ was **REJECTED** as the cornerstone (I Peter 2:7; Psalm 118:22; Matthew 21:42; Mark 12:10; Luke 20:17; Acts 4:11) and this can be seen in Masonry. Masons reject the **TRUE CORNERSTONE** and state that the Mason himself is the cornerstone.

The second degree (Fellow-Craft) reveals to the Mason that he is actually a part of God, and that God is not separate from him. Wilmshurst claims: "Happy then is the Mason who has...found God present not outside but **WITHIN HIMSELF.**"[34] This degree "is equivalent to the rite of Confirmation in the Christian Churches."[35] Another important aspect of the second degree is:

>...**ASTROLOGY,** which is one of the liberal arts and sciences recommended to the study of every Mason and the pursuit of which belongs in particular to the Fellow-Craft stage.[36]

Hutchinson writes: "Astrology was received as one of the arts which **MERITED** their patronage."[37] In spite of Biblical warnings against astrology (Deuteronomy 18:10-12; II Kings 17:17), Masonry **ENCOURAGES** it. Waite also adds that:

> …it is found…that there is astrology in modern Masonry. For example: (1) The ancient world recognised seven planets, and there are seven officers of the Lodge…. It should be added that the thesis comes from an **OCCULT** source….[38]

Master Mason is the name of the third degree. In this degree there is a very dramatic presentation where the candidate enacts a death and resurrection ceremony. When the Master Mason is raised from the "dead" he "is no longer an ordinary man, but a **DIVINIZED** man,"[39] asserts Wilmshurst. He also alleges: "He is now lord of himself; the true Master-Mason…."[40] Elsewhere he emphasizes that "the Master Mason must be his own high priest."[41] Wilmshurst, however, is not the only Mason who believes this. Anderson declares: "These Master Masons are known at different times by various names. They can be referred to as Christ and his Church…."[42] Waite maintains that "the Master-Builder of the third degree does **ACTUALLY** rise **AS** Christ…."[43]

Masonry actually is supposed to **TAKE THE PLACE OF** the church and the work of Christ upon the cross. Wilmshurst writes that Masonry "was given out to the world…as a great experiment and **MEANS OF GRACE.**"[44] Waite claims that the "Temple of Masonry is henceforward the House of Christ…."[45] Foster Bailey asks:

> May it not be true, as has been said, that if all religions and Scriptures were blotted out and only Masonry were left in the world we could still recover the great plan of salvation? Most earnestly should all true Masons consider this point….[46]

11

Masonry attempts to present a plan of salvation. Of course, to find this plan out, one must advance through numerous degrees and pay for the degrees as he advances. Several years ago $125 was required (in my community) before one could even join the Masons. But could Masonry really contain the plan of salvation? My Bible assures me that we are "not redeemed with **CORRUPTIBLE** things, as **SILVER AND GOLD**...But with the **PRECIOUS BLOOD** of Christ" (I Peter 1:18). Our salvation is **FREE,** although it certainly **WAS NOT CHEAP.** It came at a **TREMENDOUS COST** to our Savior. Yes, **SALVATION IS FREE, but FREEMASONRY IS NOT FREE!**

The first three degrees are considered to be "Craft Degrees" and they are enacted out in a "Lodge." The Lodge is arranged in a certain manner which, of course, has a special significance. Wilmshurst explains: "The East of the Lodge represents man's spirituality, his highest and most spiritual mode of consciousness"[47] and that it is "the place of the throne of the Master of all life."[48] The North, he argues, represents "the sphere of **BENIGHTEDNESS AND IGNORANCE.**"[49] Waite also believes that the North "stands in fact for **DARKNESS** according to Masonic symbolism."[50] Pike notes: "To all Masons, the North has immemorially been the place of **DARKNESS**; and of the great lights of the Lodge, none is in the North."[51] These are intriguing statements, **ESPECIALLY** when we consider that the Bible shows us that God's throne is in the **NORTH** (Psalm 48:102; Isaiah 14:12-14; Psalm 75:6-7)! So, according to Masonry, the place of God's throne is "the sphere of **BENIGHTEDNESS** and **IGNORANCE,**" and we are notified that the throne of **THEIR** Master is in the east! "The Morning Star [described by Waite as **LUCIFER**[52]] rising in the **EAST**...is an emblem to us of the ever-approaching dawn of perfection and Masonic light,"[53] confides Pike. Furthermore, one book on **WITCHCRAFT** had this caption under a picture: **"LUCIFER** is one of the multiple names of **SATAN.** As **LUCIFER** the **LIGHT-BEARER** he has **HIS HOME IN THE EAST.**"[54] **LUCIFER** is another name for **SATAN.** In fact, one **OCCULT** catalog sells a talisman called **"SATAN'S SEAL."** The description for this seal tells us that it depicts **LUCIFER** as a king and the "Inscription around the edges reads, 'Master of the abyss of **HELL.**' "[55]

The "depth" and "height" of the Lodge also have a significance. Wilmshurst indicates that the "height" represents man's **EVOLU-TION** from animal states into **GODHOOD!** In his words:

Man who has sprung from the earth and developed through the lower kingdoms of nature to his present rational state, has yet to complete his **EVOLUTION** by becoming a **GOD-LIKE BEING...**to promote which is and always has been the **SOLE AIM** and **PURPOSE** of **ALL** Initiation.[56]

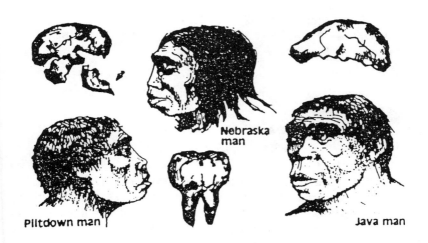

Nebraska man

Piltdown man

Java man

Here we can see that the **SOLE AIM** of Masonry is for man to be able to complete his **EVOLUTION** from the lower forms of nature into a **"GOD-LIKE BEING!"** Again, Wilmshurst is not the only proponent of this theory. Darrah likewise proclaims that man "was in the process of his **EVOLUTION** toward a **GODLIKE PERFECTION....**"[57] This is the **EXACT** promise of **SATAN** in the Garden of Eden: "Ye shall be as gods" (Genesis 3:5)! We are even told by Masonic writer, J. D. Buck, that the "only personal God Freemasonry accepts is humanity in toto...Humanity therefore is the only personal God that there is."[58] In other words, each person is God, according to Buck!

Wilmshurst continues: "To scale this 'height'...is achieved 'by the use of a ladder of many rounds or staves....' "[59] This ladder with many rounds means "that there are **INNUMERABLE PATHS** or methods by means of which men are led upwards to the spiritual Light encircling us all...."[60] The Bible specifies that there is only **ONE** way to heaven, but Masonry teaches that "there are **INNUMERABLE PATHS.**" In fact, Waite declares that "the just man...is **HIMSELF** the Ladder leading from earth to heaven."[61] This means that in

13

Masonry man is the way to heaven and not Christ! This ladder has three main rungs named Faith, Hope, and Charity. These names **SOUND** like Biblical principles, but **EVERYTHING** in the Lodge is symbolic of **SOMETHING ELSE**. These names are **NO DIF-FERENT**. Waite informs us:

> They are Aeglaea, Thalia and Euphrosyne, the Greek Charities. They have suffered **TRANSLATION** into the Christian Theological Virtues—Faith, Hope and Charity. Masonry has its part in these....[62]

Hutchinson, another Masonic writer, gives this explanation:

> The ancients used to depict the virtue Charity in the character of a **GODDESS**....

> They also represented the charities, otherwise called the Graces, under three personages...they were painted naked....[63]

We now find out that the "Greek Charities" are actually three Greek **GODDESSES** and they are usually portrayed in the nude! This hardly can compare to the Biblical virtues of Faith, Hope, and Charity! Not only do Masons worship a "Supreme Being" but we have just seen how they are also worshipping **GODDESSES** through the **SYMBOLISM** of a ladder "with many rounds." Again, we can see that Masonry is **IN CONFLICT** with the Bible for we read in Matthew 4:10: "Thou shalt worship the Lord thy God, and Him **ONLY** shalt thou serve."

Masonry also uses a line as one of its symbols. Hutchinson points out:

> This line, like Jacob's ladder, connects heaven and earth together; and by laying hold of it, we **CLIMB UP** to that place where we shall change this short line of time for the never-ending circle of eternity.[64]

Masonry insists that we **CLIMB UP** into heaven, but the Bible **SPECIFICALLY** advises us in John 10:9: "I am the **DOOR**: by Me if any man enter in, he shall be saved...." Verse 1 also explains: "Verily, verily I say unto you, he that entereth **NOT BY THE DOOR** into the sheepfold, but **CLIMBETH UP** some other way, the same is a thief and a robber." Masonry cannot be the way to Jesus Christ because Masons **THEMSELVES** contend that "we **CLIMB UP** to that place" and they refuse to enter in by the door which is Jesus Christ.

In the 17th degree (Knight of the East and West) we see **BLASPHEMY** and **DISOBEDIENCE** to Scriptural commands. This degree, recounts Waite,

> ...is sealed with the blood of the Candidate, who is lanced slightly on the arms...as if...he were somehow taking the part of the Mystic Lamb who was slain and so "redeemed us to God" by His blood....On the pedestal before him there is a Bible, to the markers of which are attached seven seals, like the mysterious Book in the APOCALYSE [Revelation].... These seals are opened or broken successively.[65]

The sacred word of this ritual is **"ABADDON."**[66] Now, let's notice a few points about this degree. **1)** The Candidate **TAKES THE PLACE OF CHRIST** by shedding his own blood. **2)** The Candidate is lanced on the arms but the Bible tells us not to make any cuttings in our flesh (Leviticus 21:5). This warning was for a purpose for C. J. S. Thompson mentions: "Pacts with the devil were said to be always signed by the executor with his blood as being the most sacred seal."[67] **3)** The seven seals of Revelation are opened. Again, **SOMEONE ELSE** is taking Christ's place for **ONLY** Christ was **WORTHY** to open these seals. In Revelation 5:2 we read that an angel asked **"WHO** is worthy to open the book, and to loose the seals thereof?" Verse 3 cautions us that **"NO MAN** in heaven, **NOR IN EARTH,** neither under the earth, was able to **OPEN** the book." John then "wept much, because **NO MAN** was found **WORTHY TO OPEN** and to read the book, neither **TO LOOK THEREON"** (verse 4). Then, verse 5 specifies that the **ONLY ONE** who was able to **OPEN** the seals was **CHRIST.** Christ **ALONE** is **WORTHY** to open these seals, but Masons act out this passage and open the seals, proving **ONCE MORE** that the Mason is **ACTUALLY** taking the place of Christ! **4)** The sacred word given is **"ABADDON."** This is interesting for Revelation 9:11 reveals that the demons in hell "had a king over them, which is the angel of the bottomless pit, whose name in the Hebrew tongue is **ABADDON....**" **ABADDON** was the king over the demons, yet the Masons believe that **ABADDON** is a "sacred word!" In the next chapter we will learn who the **TRUE GOD** of Masonry **REALLY** is. When you discover who the god of Masonry is, you should be able to see why they consider **ABADDON** a **SACRED NAME!**

2. WHO IS THE GOD OF MASONRY?

Masons emphasize that to participate in the Masonic rituals one **MUST** believe in a "Supreme Being." "Freemasonry is available to any man of good character who believes in a Supreme Being and is closed only to avowed atheists and agnostics,"[1] claims Ralph Anderson. Since the Bible cautions us that "Thou shalt worship the Lord thy God and Him **ONLY** shalt thou serve" (Matthew 4:10) and the Masons worship a Supreme Being, is this Supreme Being the **SAME** God as the Christians worship or is he a **DIFFERENT** god? As you read on you will find out who this "Supreme Being" is, but this "Supreme Being" is not the **ONLY** god Masons worship! Although many Masons may be **UNAWARE** of the **POLYTHEISM** in Masonry, **MANY** gods and goddesses are worshipped through the **SYMBOLISM AND RITUALS** of Masonry. One poem, written by a Mason, J. S. M. Ward, sums up some of the **MYTHOLOGY** that is **PREVALENT** in Masonry.

> Bacchus died and rose again,
>> On the Golden Syrian Plain;
>
> Osiris rose from out his grave;
>> And thereby mankind did save;
>
> Adonis likewise shed his blood
>> By the yellow Syrian flood,
>
> Zoroaster brought to birth
>> Mithra from his cave of earth
>
> And we to-day in Christian Lands
>> We with them can join hands.[2]

Bacchus, Osiris, Adonis, and Mithra are all **GODS** that are worshipped by **OCCULTISTS** and **MASONS!** Of course, these are just a **FEW** of the **GODS** that are actually worshipped through different Masonic ceremonies. It doesn't matter to the Mason that God proclaims: "Thou shalt worship the Lord thy God and Him **ONLY** shalt thou serve" (Matthew 4:10).

Osiris is the Egyptian god of the dead as well as a **SUN-GOD** but he is also known by many other names. In Thrace and Greece he is known as **DIONYSUS,** the god of pleasures and of partying and wine. Festivals held in his honor often resulted in **HUMAN SACRIFICES AND ORGIASTIC** (sexual) rites.[3] In Rome he is called **LIBER** or

BACCHUS. The Lydians label him **BASSAREUS** and in Persia he is identified as **MITHRAS,** where **ASTROLOGY** is practiced by his followers. He is **ZAGREUS** to the Cretans and "became an underworld divinity who welcomed the souls of the dead to Hades and helped with their purification,"[4] declares Paul Hamlyn. He also informs us that since Zagreus was killed and resurrected (in mythology) he "became the symbol of everlasting life."[5] The Phrygians know Osiris as **SABAZIUS** where he is honored as a solar deity (a sun god) who was represented by horns and his emblem was a **SERPENT!**[6]. In other places he went by other names such as **Deouis, The Boy Jupiter, The Centaur, Orion, The Boy Plutus, Iswara, The Winged One, Nimrod, Adoni, Hermes, Prometheus, Poseidon, Butes, Dardanus, Himeros, Imbros, Iasius, Zeus, Iacchus, Hu, Thor, Bel, Serapis, Ormuzd, Apollo, Thammuz, Atus, Hercules,** and, believe it or not, **BAAL!** Most of these gods were considered to be solar deities or sun-gods. The **WORSHIP OF THE SUN,** disguised through the use of gods and symbols, plays a **VERY IMPORTANT** role in Masonry!

It is to this god, Osiris (under the name of Hiram Abiff), that the Masons pay honor in the third degree. The **DRAMA** for this degree (Master Mason) involves a death and resurrection ceremony. The Master-Mason-to-be is said to be working on Solomon's Temple. He is in possession of the name of God (the "Lost Word" of Masonry) and he has promised to reveal this to the other workers when the Temple is finished. Since the wages are higher for those who possess this name, the other workers become jealous and insist that he **REVEAL THE NAME** to them **BEFORE** the Temple is finished. When he refuses to do so, three angry ruffians kill him and hastily bury him. Eventually his grave is discovered and, after the third attempt, he is raised to life again. The first word he spoke is the **SUBSTITUTE** for the "Lost Word" and it is this word that is said to be passed down to Master Masons today.[7]

Any one who is familiar with Egyptian mythology should be able to see the correlation between the myth of Hiram Abiff and of the

18

Egyptian god, Osiris. Pierson contends: "We readily recognize in Hiram Abiff the Osiris of the Egyptians...."[8] "In Egypt the dead man was identified with Osiris, and addressed as Osiris."[9] Waite acknowledges that:

> There is **NO QUESTION** that the **MYTH** of Osiris covers the **WHOLE STORY** of mystical life and is presented in the Funerary Ritual [the death and resurrection ceremony of the third degree] as the soul's own story. There is no more eloquent valediction to the departing soul than that which says: Thou hast gone living to Osiris. The promise is life in Osiris. The great doctrine, the great revelation of all the true Mysteries is that Osiris lives.... We also as Masons **LOOK FORWARD TO UNION** of the departed with Osiris....[10]

These Masonic authors realize that the ceremonies are only based on **MYTHS** or **FABLES**. *Collier's Encyclopedia* states: "Masonry fosters an elaborate **MYTHOLOGY...**"[11] but since they have turned away from the truth, there is only the **FALSE** left. W. L. Wilmshurst, a Mason, points out:

> It **MATTERS NOTHING** whether the prototype be one whose historical actuality and identity can be demonstrated, or whether he can be regarded **ONLY** as **LEGENDARY** or **MYTHICAL**....In Egypt the prototype was Osiris, who was slain by his malignant brother Typhon, but whose mangled limbs were collected in a coffer from which he emerged reintegrated and **DIVINIZED**. In Greece the prototype was Bacchus, who was torn to pieces by the Titans. Baldur in Scandinavia and Mithra in Graeco-Roman Europe were similar prototypes. In Masonry the prototype is Hiram Abiff....[12]

Many Masons believe that they are acting out the death and resurrection ritual of Christ. Even if this were the case, which it is not, this ritual would be blasphemous for a Christian, but these Masons are actually acting out the **MYTH** of Osiris and Isis, two **PAGAN** deities of Egypt. Isis was considered to be "supreme in **MAGICAL** power..."[13] and "she was the goddess of...**MAGIC**."[14] Osiris committed incest by marrying his sister, Isis, so those portraying him are not very righteous characters, are they? Also, several symbols in the Lodge that Masons should readily recognize are the Sun, the point within a circle, the Tau Cross, and the All-Seeing Eye—all symbols representing Osiris![15] We will look at these symbols closer and see what they mean in the next chapter.

Not only do Masons rely on **FABLES,** but they also **TAKE THE PLACE** of Christ. In the 19th degree of the Scottish Rite, called "Grand Pontiff," Masons attend a pageant in which part of the book of Revelation is enacted. Waite recounts this drama:

> Amidst darkness and isolation thereafter the officers of the Chapter proclaim the dominion of the beast, the opening of the seven vials of REVELATION and the fall of Babylon.... The Candidate is brought into light and is shewn the four-square city coming down out of Heaven...while He who sits upon the throne, **THOUGH** He is **CALLED** the Lord God Almighty and Redeemer, **IS NOT** the Christ of St. John.... The Candidate is anointed with oil, is made and proclaimed a priest for ever according to the Order of Melchizedek.... The New Jerusalem is interpreted as Ancient Masonry.[16]

Although Delmar Darrah, a 33rd degree Mason, assures us that "there **NEVER** has been **ANY CONFLICT** between the church and Freemasonry,"[17] we can see several points of **CONFLICT** between the pageantry of the degree of Grand Pontiff and the Bible. First we notice that the person who sits on the throne is **CALLED** "the Lord God Almighty and Redeemer," but he **"IS NOT** the Christ of St. John." If he **IS NOT** the Christ of the Bible, then who is he? Read on and you will discover who the god of Masonry **REALLY** is! Secondly, we see that the Mason is anointed with oil and proclaimed "a priest for ever according to the Order of Melchizedek." Hebrews 5:5 and 9 clearly states that "Christ glorified **NOT** Himself to be made an high priest" but was "called **OF GOD** an high priest after the order of Melchizedek," but Masons glorify **THEMSELVES** and take **ON THEMSELVES** the honor of the priesthood that was given to Christ **ALONE.** Thirdly, notice that Masons interpret the "New Jerusalem" as "Ancient Masonry!"

The 25th degree of the Scottish Rite is called "Knight of the Brazen Serpent." Again Waite describes this degree and reveals to us that the twelve signs of the Zodiac are illustrated and a Tau Cross, encompassed by a **SERPENT,** is in the **EAST.** The Master retires to call upon God and then

> ...returns bearing a **SYMBOL OF SALVATION,** being a Brazen **SERPENT** entwined about the Tau Cross.... It is given thereafter to the Candidate, as a symbol of faith, repentance and mercy.[18]

Again we can see conflict between the degrees of Masonry and the Bible. The Bible warns against astrology, yet the Lodge is set up in such a way as to correspond with the twelve signs of the Zodiac, which is astrology. We also notice that the symbol of salvation is the "Brazen **SERPENT!**" Once again Christ is set aside for **ANOTHER** symbol of salvation. The Bible specifies that the **SERPENT** represents **SATAN,** but Masonry uses the **SERPENT** as a **SYMBOL OF SALVATION!**

In conjunction with the **SERPENT,** let's look at the Masonic apron. Wilmshurst writes: "Brethren, I charge you to regard your **APRON** as one of the **MOST PRECIOUS** and speaking symbols our Order has to give you."[19] I find this statement **QUITE INTRIGUING.** When Adam and Eve sinned they sewed together an apron of fig leaves. We find, however, that God **WAS NOT PLEASED** with the **APRONS** and He made them **COATS** of skin to **CLOTHE** them (Genesis 3:7, 21), but Waite indicates that "in Craft Masonry and its connection the **APRON** is the **ONLY PROPER AND POSSIBLE CLOTHING.**"[20]

In the first degree of Masonry the candidate is given an unadorned white apron which indicates purity of soul.[21] In the second degree blue rosettes are added to the apron to indicate that progress has been made in regeneration.[22] In the third degree Wilmshurst explains that

> ...still further progress is emblematized by the increased blue adornments of the Apron, as also by its silver tassels and the silver **SERPENT** used to fasten the apronstrings.... The silver **SERPENT** is the **EMBLEM OF DIVINE WISDOM** knitting the soul's new-made vesture together.[23]

The newly initiated Mason is instructed that his white apron is the **"MOST PRECIOUS"** symbol of Masonry and that it represents purity. We must remember, however, that this apron is a **SYMBOL.** What, then, is the **REAL MEANING BEHIND** this object? To find out we must return to **MYTHOLOGY.** Pike notes that the god Jupiter

Ammon's picture was painted with the sign of the Ram or Lamb.[24] He mentions that Jupiter Ammon is "the **SAME AS OSIRIS,** Adoni, Adonis, Atys, and the other **SUN-GODS....**"[25] Hutchinson also notes that Jupiter Ammon is "painted with horns"[26] and that he is the "same as **BAAL** or **MOLOCH....**[and] Adonis, whom some ancient authors call **OSIRIS.**"[27] His ceremonies "consisted in clothing the Initiate with the skin of a white lamb. And in this we see the **ORIGIN** of the **APRON** of white sheep-skin **USED IN MASONRY.**"[28] So, the **APRON** was used in connection with the ceremonies of Osiris and this apron is the **"ONLY PROPER"** clothing, according to Waite.

Also notice that in the third degree a **SERPENT** is added to the **APRON** and that it is an emblem of **DIVINE WISDOM!** The *Entered Apprentice's Handbook* points out that

> ...the Serpent is regarded as "the Shining One"—the Holy Wisdom itself. Thus we see that the Serpent on our apron denotes that we are encircled by the Holy Wisdom....

> The snake is peculiarly associated with [the Hindu god] Shiva, the Destroyer, whose close symbolic association with the third [Masonic] degree is obvious...He is depicted making the...[sign] of a Master Mason.[29]

Another god, **SHIVA,** is now introduced into the **PANTHEON** of Masonry. Shiva (or Siva) has numerous wives and

> ...wanders naked about the countryside on his white bull Nandi, overindulging in drugs, and encouraging starvation and self-mutilation. The innermost sanctuaries of Shiva temples always feature a lingam, the stylized erect phallus which symbolizes his rampant sexuality.[30]

The **SERPENT** is quite prevalent and important in Masonry. When Jim Shaw, a former Mason who is now a Christian, went to the Temple to receive his 33rd degree, he reported:

> ...the thing that is most noticeable is the way the walls are decorated with **SERPENTS.** There are all kinds; some very long and large. **MANY** of the Scottish Rite degrees include the representation of **SERPENTS** and I recognized them among those decorating the walls.[31]

Albert Pike devotes page after page of his book to the prevalence and worship of **SERPENTS.** He discloses that "The Phoenicians called the **SERPENT** agathodemon [the **GOOD** spirit]...."[32] "In reality, the hawk-headed **SERPENT,** genius of **LIGHT,** or **GOOD** genius, was the symbol of the **SUN.**[33] "The horned **SERPENT** was the hieroglyphic for a God."[34]

Two other names for Osiris are Bel and Hu. Pike relates to us that "The Greeks called Bel Beliar; and Hesychius interprets that word to mean a **DRAGON** or great **SERPENT**"[35] and "The British God Hu was called 'The **DRAGON**—Ruler of the World,' and his car was drawn by **SERPENTS.**"[36] Statements like these are interesting because in the Bible we read that "the great **DRAGON** was cast out, that old **SERPENT,** called the **DEVIL,** and **SATAN,** which **DECEIVETH** the whole world..." (Revelation 12:9).

Other connections to Satan can be found. Pike, writing about the pagan god Thor, reveals that "Thor was the **SUN,** the Egyptian **OSIRIS** and Kneph, the Phoenician Bel or **BAAL.**"[37] Bel (or Baal) was believed to be the "lord of the air"[38] as well as a sun-god.[39] Remember also that the god **BAAL** is a synonym for the **DEVIL.**[40] Baal "had the body of a spider and three heads—those of a man, a toad and a cat."[41] This god, under the name of Thor, is called "the Prince of the Power of the Air."[42] Baal worship is condemned by the Bible (I Kings 16:30-33, 22:53; II Kings 17:16, etc.), and in Ephesians we find that **SATAN** is called the "prince of the power of the air." Not only does **SATAN** have the same title as is given to the god Thor, but we should notice that the word "Thor" means "thunder."[43] Thor "was the god of lightning and thunder in Norse mythology."[44] This is a significant statement for **SATANISTS** use the lightning bolt as a symbol of **SATAN.** Satanic rock groups also use the symbol called a "Satanic S," which resembles a lightning bolt and is probably taken from the reference in Luke 10:18 where Jesus says: "I beheld Satan as lightning fall from heaven."[45] One of these Satanic rock groups called KISS ("the name stands for 'Knights in Satan's Service' "[46]) has a song on one of their albums entitled "God of Thunder." This song claims:

I was raised by the demons
Trained to reign as the one
God of Thunder and Rock and Roll
The sound you're under
Will slowly rob you of your virgin soul.
I'm the Lord of the Wasteland
A modern day man of steel
I gather darkness to please me,
I command you to kneel
Before the god of thunder
The god of rock and roll.[47]

This god is obviously Satan. Is it any wonder that the Bible further informs us that this "prince of the power of the air" is "the spirit that now worketh in the children of **DISOBEDIENCE...**" (Ephesians 2:2)?

Since the gods of Masonry (Thor, Baal, Shiva, Pan, Osiris, etc.) actually **REPRESENT SATAN** in different camouflages and since the **SERPENT** is widespread in Masonry and the Bible clearly states that the **SERPENT** is **SATAN,** we see that the Masons are in **ACTUALITY** worshipping **SATAN (LUCIFER).** Of course, Masonic writers themselves **PLAINLY** confess to us who they worship! **WHO** is it? It is none other than **SATAN (LUCIFER)!** Hutchinson gives the following comment about the fall of man:

But, alas, he [Adam] fell! By disobedience, he forfeited all his glory and felicity; and, **WONDERFUL TO RECOUNT** in the midst of this **EXALTED** state, **SATAN PREVAILED.**[48]

The footnote on this sentence gives this explanation: "Thus originated the introduction of a **SERPENT** among the **SYMBOLS OF FREEMASONRY....** Serpent-worship derives its origin from the

SAME SOURCE."[49] Another footnote elsewhere in this book is a quote from *Key to the New Testament,* which states, in part:

> The corruptions flowing from the Egyptian philosophy, when adapted to Christianity, were these:—they held that the God of the Jews was the Demiurgus...that the **SERPENT** who deceived Eve **OUGHT TO BE HONOURED** for endeavoring to rescue men from their slavery to the Demiurgus.[50]

Pike brags:

> ...Lucifer, the *Light-bearer!* Strange and mysterious name to give to the Spirit of Darkness! Lucifer, the Son of the Morning! Is it *he* who bears the *Light...?* Doubt it not [emphasis in the original]![51]

Masonic testimony is clear that the **SERPENT** or **SATAN** (Lucifer) should be worshipped. In fact, the "Lost Word" of Masonry has to do with Satan. Masons have been in search of a so-called "Lost Word," which is supposed to be the **REAL** name of God, but has been lost. In the third degree the Mason is given a **SUBSTITUTE** word and told to look "to that bright and Morning Star...."[52] Waite suggests that the Word revealed in the third degree "was of similar value to our old friend **ABRACADABRA**."[53] He mentions elsewhere that

> ...since the sphere of Ritual is also a sphere of **SORCERY,** on proceeding to initiation he is given the symbol **ABRACADABRA**...and is told it is the **TRUE WORD**.[54]

```
A B R A C A D A B R A
A B R A C A D A B R
A B R A C A D A B
A B R A C A D A
A B R A C A D
A B R A C A
A B R A C
A B R A
A B R
A B
A
```

Most people know that the word **ABRACADABRA** has to do with **MAGIC,** but did you know that this word comes from **ABRAXAS?**[55] **ABRAXAS,** by the way, is a **DEMON!** Masons are actually taught that this **DEMON** is the **TRUE WORD.** However, this word is only a **SUBSTITUTE.** Then, in the 13th degree (Royal Arch) he is given the name of the "Lost Word" of Masonry. Let's see, first of all, who is the **"BRIGHT AND MORNING STAR"** and then let's look at the "Lost Word" and **WHO** is represented thereby.

Revelation 22:16 explains: "I Jesus...am the root and offspring of David, and the **BRIGHT AND MORNING STAR."** Now, do the Masons worship Jesus as the "bright and Morning Star?" There are several reasons why this answer is **"NO!"** One reason is that **EVERYTHING** in the Lodge is **SYMBOLICAL** of **SOMETHING ELSE,** so if the "bright and Morning Star" is Christ in reality, it is only a **SYMBOL** to the Mason. In addition, Wilmshurst admits that "Hebrew Biblical names **REPRESENT NOT** persons, but **PER-SONIFICATIONS** of spiritual principles...."[56]

There is a greater reason, however, that we know that the "bright and Morning Star" **IS NOT** Christ, and that is from Masonic testimony. Waite, describing one picture in his book, analyzes it like this:

> There is a globe in her right hand on which is balanced a Genius, holding a torch, and said to typify the **MORNING STAR OR LUCIFER....** From a Masonic point of view, the symbol in its plenary sense is the coming forth of conquering **LIGHT.**[57]

Masonic testimony points out that the **MORNING STAR IS LUCIFER** and that this symbol represents the "coming forth of conquering light." So, when Masons speak of the light of Masonry they are actually referring to **LUCIFER** bringing forth the light. Lucifer, as you may already know, means "Light Bearer" or "Light Bringer!" The Bible also informs us that Satan (Lucifer) comes as "an angel of light" (II Corinthians 11:14).

As mentioned earlier, another name for Osiris is Mithras. According to *The World Book Encyclopedia,* Mithras "was an **ANGEL OF LIGHT** who fought on the side of the god Ahura-Mazda.... The Zoroastrian scriptures called Mithras 'the Heavenly Light.' "[58] He was also identified with the **SUN.**[59] The mention of Ahura-Mazda is interesting for it is **THIS** god that the lecture of the 32nd degree of Masonry deals with. In this lecture Ahura-Mazda is called the "spirit of light."[60] The Masons are then instructed to:

Look to the East, my brothers...and behold the seven-pointed star, the great symbol of this degree, with the seven colors of the rainbow. The seven colors and seven points represent the seven potencies of Ahura.

Observe now the great Delta of Pythagoras consisting of 36 lights arranged in eight rows to form an equilateral triangle. The light of the apex of the Delta represents Ahura-Mazda, source of all light.[61]

The lecture continues and the Masons are told that the "triliteral name for god is composed of"[62] three Hindu gods: Brahma, Vishnu, and Siva. Siva (or Shiva), by the way, is a **SYNONYM** for **SATAN!** In fact, Anton LaVey, founder of the Church of Satan, lists Shiva, Lucifer, and Pan (among others) in his *Satanic Bible* as **SYNONYMS FOR SATAN!**[63]

LUCIFER, then, is the god honored and revered by Masons as the **TRUE GOD!** J. Edward Decker, Jr., gives us a quote from Albert Pike, a 33rd degree Mason. On July 14, 1889, Pike gave instructions to the 23 Supreme Councils of the World:

That which we must say to the crowd is—We worship a God, but it is the God that one adores without superstition.

To you, Sovereign Grand Inspectors General [the name of the 33rd degree, the highest degree in Scottish Rite Masonry], we say this, that you may repeat it to the Brethren of the 32nd, 31st, and 30th degrees—The Masonic Religion should be, by all of us initiates of the high degrees, maintained in the purity of the **LUCIFERIAN DOCTRINE....**

Yes, **LUCIFER IS GOD....**

...the **PURE** philosophical **RELIGION IS THE BELIEF IN LUCIFER...LUCIFER, GOD OF LIGHT AND GOD OF GOOD....**[64]

With this admission, is it any wonder that Pike is called the "Pontiff of **LUCIFERIAN** Freemasonry?"[65] In addition, he is adored by Masonic authors such as Waite, who brags: "I believe...his name will be...of **PRECIOUS MEMORY** in **ALL** American Masonry."[66] In fact, *Morals and Dogma,* a book written by Pike is the handbook for Masons. When Jim Shaw earned his 32nd degree, he, as well as the others present, were given

...a copy of Albert Pike's book.... We were told that it was *the* source book for Freemasonry and its meaning. We were also told that it must never leave our possession, and that arrangements must be made so that upon our deaths it would be returned to the Scottish Rite [emphasis in the original].[67]

Also, C. Fred Kleinknecht, a 33rd degree Mason,

...told all Masons this last January that one particular book was to be their daily guide for living—their "Bible." That book, said Kleinknecht, is Albert Pike's *Morals and Dogma*.[68]

The **MAJORITY** of Masons in the first few degrees **ARE NOT AWARE** of the god of Masonry, yet Hutchinson boasts that "the first state of a Mason is representative of the **FIRST STAGE** of worship of the **TRUE GOD**."[69] He highly insinuates that those **OUTSIDE** of the Masonic ranks **ARE NOT** worshipping the **TRUE GOD!** The Masons have been taught that this **TRUE GOD** is called the "Grand Architect of the Universe" and that **ANYONE** who believes in a Supreme Being may join Masonry. They have been advised that there is **NO CONFLICT** between Christianity and Masonry. To hide the fact of who their god is, those entering Masonry must enact strange rituals and only **AFTER** the Candidate has completed the 13th degree is he told the name of the "Lost Word." Why must this word be kept secret for **SO LONG?** The answer is that if the word and its meaning were revealed to the Candidate in the beginning, he most likely **WOULD HAVE NEVER JOINED UP!**

What is the "Lost Word?" Waite indicates that the "Lost Word" has to do with Wisdom and that "Wisdom in this case is a **SYNONYM** of the Word...."[70] Before I give you the "Lost Word" let me remind you that Wilmshurst claims that the **"SERPENT** is the emblem of **DIVINE WISDOM"**[71] and the Lost Word is a **SYNONYM** for Wisdom, so this Word has to do with the **SERPENT!** Well, the secret Word is "Jao-Bul-On." You may wonder, "What does **THAT** mean?" "Jao" is the Chaldean name for God. "Bul" is a Syriac word which means "Baal," who was a Canaanite fertility god associated with **LICENTIOUS** rites and **MAGIC**.[72] Baal is actually another name for the Devil![73] "On" is the Egyptian word signifying "Osiris," the god of the underworld.[74] So, here again, we can see Satan is deified and **HONORED** by the Masons. We are told further (in the ritual of the 13th degree) that this "triune essence of the Deity"[75] represents "His creative, preservative, and de-creative powers."[76] This sentence gives a **VERY VIVID** description of the Hindu gods. In the **PAGAN** religion of Hinduism we also see a "trinity" of three gods—Brahma, the creator; Vishnu, the preserver; and Shiva, the destroyer. Waite explains: "Siva [or Shiva] is the Babylonian Bel, **IDENTICAL** with the **SUN-GOD** I A O...."[77] *The World Book Encyclopedia* states that Bel is "another name for the god Baal,"[78] and Baal is another name for Satan, so Satan is being worshipped through the Masonic ritual, for Shiva, the god with "de-creative powers," is **ANOTHER** name for Satan!

One more name for Satan is Pan. "He was half man and half goat..."[79] and he is "usually shown with goat feet, curly hair, short horns, and a beard."[80] An **OCCULT** catalog from International Imports mentions: "In Greek mythology Pan was the **GOD OF NATURE**....He is also equated with **SATAN** and life's baser aspects."[81] **ONCE AGAIN** we can see that Masonry honors **SATAN** for Hutchinson confesses: "The knowledge of the **GOD OF NATURE** forms the **FIRST ESTATE** of our profession...."[82] He also points out that the God of Nature was adored under the names of Osiris and Isis (the wife/sister of Osiris).[83]

Yes, **LUCIFER (SATAN)** is the **GOD OF MASONRY** and the so-called "God of Light." Wilmshurst tries to convince us that:

> Christian and Masonic doctrine are **IDENTICAL** in intention though different in method. The one says "Via Crucis"; the other "Via Lucis"; yet the two ways are but one way.[84]

"Via Crucis" means "by way of the Cross" and "Via Lucis" means "by way of light." These two ways **CANNOT** be **IDENTICAL.** One way follows the way of the Cross of Christ which leads to heaven; the other follows the way of the light of Lucifer which leads to hell. Isn't it plain to see which path the Masons are on?

3. SYMBOLS OF MASONRY

Now that we have discovered who the **REAL** god of Masonry is, let's look at some of the Masonic symbols and see how these symbols actually represent their god. Arthur Waite states:

> The grand and universal symbols which are characteristic of Emblematic Freemasonry are the Pentalpha or Pentagram, the Hexangular Seal of Solomon—called otherwise Shield of David— the All-Seeing Eye, the Point within a Circle, the Cubic Stone, the Sun and Moon. The particular symbols...are the Rough and Perfect Ashlar, and of course the Working Tools. There is finally the Blazing Star.[1]

Let's look at a few of these symbols in more detail. The pentalpha or pentagram is a five-pointed star. It is used in all kinds of **MAGIC** rituals. Sybil Leek, a well-known **WITCH,** declares that the "pentagram **HAS ALWAYS** been used in ritual **MAGIC** and in the **WITCHCRAFT** rites of healing."[2] Mr. Wedeck explains:

> The pentacle [pentagram], the five-pointed figure, contained mystic symbols, used especially in **DIVINATION** and the **CONJURATION OF SPIRITS.** The pentalpha, a design formed by interlacing five A's, was also in similar use. To summon **DEMONIAC** help, the pentagram was fashioned: a five-pointed geometric figure.[3]

International Imports produces an **OCCULT** catalog. This company sells altar covers with pentagrams on them—a "**CIRCLED PENTAGRAM** for **WHITE MAGIC OCCULT** work; **INVERTED PENTAGRAM** for **BLACK MAGIC** rituals."[4] The "inverted pentagram" is the five-pointed star with one point **DOWN.** Elsewhere this catalog advertises **OCCULT** jewelry with a pentagram. It adds that the pentagram is the "**MOST POWERFUL OF ALL OCCULT** talismans.... It is alleged that it is **MORE POWERFUL** than the cross...."[5] We are told that the inverted pentagram is "a sign for evil."[6]

Texe Marrs informs us:

> Celtic priests called it [the pentagram] the witch's foot. In the Middle Ages it became known in Britain and elsewhere in Europe as the goblin's cross, devil's sign, and the wizard's star. Among the druids of Great Britain, it was the blasphemous sign of the Godhead.[7]

Manly P. Hall, a 33rd degree Mason and an **OCCULTIST,** points out that the

> ...pentagram is used extensively in **BLACK MAGIC,** but when so used its form always differs in one of three ways: The star may be broken at one point by not permitting the converging lines to touch; it may be inverted by having one point down and two up; or it may be distorted by having the points of varying length.

> When used in **BLACK MAGIC,** the pentagram is called "the sign of the cloven hoof," or the footprint of the devil. The star with two points upward is also called the "Goat of Mendes," because the inverted star is the same shape as a goat's head. When the upright star turns and the upper point falls to the bottom, it signifies the fall of the Morning Star.[8]

As stated, the pentagram can be drawn with one point down or two points down. **WITCHES, SATANISTS,** and **MASONS ALL** use this symbol! Satanists the world over use the pentagram with one point down and witches use the pentagram with two points down. Gary Jennings, in his book, *Black Magic, White Magic,* reveals that

> ...the most powerful and respected of all **MAGICAL SYM-BOLS** was the pentagram—the figure of five sides and five angles.... The belief was that if this figure were drawn with a single angle...pointing down, the **SIGN REPRESENTED SATAN** and thus was used for invoking evil spirits.[9]

Max Wood states: "If you are a member of the Satanist Church, you wear one [a pentagram]."[10] With this in mind I was intrigued when I discovered that the **EASTERN STAR** (a **MASONIC** organization composed of third degree Masons and women relatives of third degree Masons[11]) uses the pentagram with the **ONE POINT DOWN**—the **SAME SYMBOL** that the **SATANISTS** use! The Mystic Shrine (another **MASONIC** group composed only of Masons who have advanced to the 32nd degree) also uses a pentagram with **ONE POINT DOWN** as its symbol. C. J. S. Thompson, in *The Mysteries and Secrets of Magic,* mentions that in India the pentacle "is the symbol of Siva and Brahman"[12] and Siva (or Shiva) is **ANOTHER** name for **SATAN,** so the pentacle (or pentagram) is one of **SATAN'S** symbols. It's no wonder, then, that Satanists use it.

Dick Sutphen, an **OPENLY CONFESSED** New Ager, uses the pentacle in his **MAGICAL RITUALS.** He confirms that the "pentacle [or pentagram] holds an **IMPORTANT PLACE IN RITUAL MAGIC"**[13] and that the

> ...history of man is the history of magic, and it has been practiced from earliest times through Druidism, the Magi, the Egyptians, Greeks, Romans, Jews, Knight Templar [a **MASONIC** organization], Order of the Golden Dawn and in various organizations right up to the present.[14]

Sutphen lists many groups that are adept in **MAGIC.** I find it **VERY FASCINATING** that the **MASONS** claim the **SAME** sources for their knowledge of Masonry. Hutchinson acknowledges that "our mode of teaching the principles of our profession [Masonry] is derived from the **DRUIDS...**[and] our chief emblems originally [came] from Egypt...."[15] He notifies us that a few select men who had "the light of understanding and truth"[16] were

> ...under the denomination of **MAGI** among the Persians; wise men, **SOOTHSAYERS** and **ASTROLOGERS,** among the Chaldeans; philosophers among the Greeks and Romans; **BRAHMINS** among the Indians; **DRUIDS** and **BARDS** among the Britons....[17]

Hutchinson also brags "that we [Masonry] retain more of the ceremonials and doctrines of the **DRUIDS** than is to be found in the whole world besides...."[18] The **DRUIDS** were **OCCULT** priests who **WORSHIPPED MANY GODS,** practiced **ASTROLOGY,** and offered **HUMAN SACRIFICES.** So, **BY MASONIC TESTIMONY,** Masonry is founded on the principles of **MAGIC** and **OCCULTISM!** It should be plain, then, that Masonry **IS AN OCCULT RELIGION** and **IS NOT** compatible **AT ALL** with Biblical Christianity!

Another Masonic symbol is the **ALL-SEEING EYE.** We are assured that this represents the all-seeing-eye of God, but this, too, is a **SYMBOL** that has a **DEEPER** meaning than what is normally revealed. Pike, the 33rd degree Mason who **BOASTED** that "Lucifer is God,"[19] explains in his book:

> Masonry, like all the religions, all the Mysteries, Hermeticism and Alchemy, **CONCEALS ITS SECRETS** from all except the Adepts and Sages or the Elect, and uses **FALSE EXPLANA-TIONS AND MISINTERPRETATIONS** of its symbols to **MISLEAD** those who deserve only to be misled, to conceal the Truth, which it calls Light, from them, and to draw them away from it.[20]

Nonetheless, if one does enough research, it is possible to find out **WHO** the all-seeing-eye **REALLY** represents. International Imports mentions that the all-seeing-eye is the **THIRD EYE OF CLAIRVOYANCE.**[21] Clairvoyance is a form of **DIVINATION** and the Bible **SPECIFICAL-LY** warns us not to practice **ANY FORM OF DIVINATION** (Deuteronomy 18:10-12, etc.). J. Edward Decker, Jr. reports that " 'The All Seeing Eye' is a **MASONIC** representation of Osiris."[22] Osiris is the Egyptian god of the dead (and of the underworld) and part of the "Masonic trinity" to whom Masons pay honor.

The Blazing Star is related to the pentagram. Waite reports: "The Blazing Star is a **MASONIC** variant of the Pentagram."[23] Pike reveals that the "Blazing Star **IN OUR LODGES...**has been regarded as an emblem of Omniscience, or the **ALL-SEEING EYE,** which to the Ancients was the **SUN.**"[24] The Blazing Star is also claimed to be "an emblem of the Sacred Name of God and thus of God Himself...."[25] What is the name of **THIS** God? Pike remarks that this symbol was "the emblem of **OSIRIS,** the Creator."[26] He reiterates that **OSIRIS'** "...power was symbolized by an Eye over a Sceptre. The Sun was termed by the Greeks the Eye of Jupiter, and the Eye of the World; and his is the **ALL-SEEING EYE IN OUR LODGES.**"[27] It is quite clear, then, that the **ALL-SEEING EYE** in the Masonic Lodges is actually a symbol of **SATAN!** In addition, we are told that this **ALL-SEEING EYE** can represent **SHIVA,** a **SYNONYM** for **SATAN,**[28] so, **EITHER WAY** Satan is being represented in the Lodge by the symbol of the **ALL-SEEING EYE!**

The hexagram (also called the Shield of David, Star of David, Crest of Solomon, and Hexangular Seal of Solomon) is another symbol used by **MASONS, WITCHES,** and **MAGICIANS.** Jennings indicates that the hexagram, although used now as a symbol of the Jewish religion, was used **LONG BEFORE** Judaism.[29] He notes that the sign was used as a

> ...stand-by for **MAGICIANS** and **ALCHEMISTS.** The **SORCERERS** believed it represented the footprint of a special kind of **DEMON** called a **TRUD** and used it in ceremonies both to **CALL UP DEMONS** and to keep them away.[30]

Spellbound, a book written by Jack Chick, points out:

> ...in witchcraft this [the hexagram] is the **MOST EVIL SIGN** in the occult world. It must be present to call a demon forth during a ceremonial rite. The word hex, meaning to place a curse on someone, comes from this emblem.[31]

Waite confesses that the hexagram is the sign of the Grand Architect.[32] Those entering Masonry are taught that the Grand Architect represents God, but you must remember that the Masonic god is actually **LUCIFER!** The hexagram, therefore, is another symbol of **LUCIFER (SATAN).**

Masonry also uses the sun symbol. The symbol for the sun is usually represented as a circle, signifying Deity. Jennings, expounding on **MAGICAL SYMBOLS,** informs us that the

> ...oldest diagram in use was the simple circle, the shape of the all-powerful sun...and the all-seeing eye's iris. The idea of eternity was often symbolized by a **SERPENT** coiled into a perfect circle, biting its own tail.[33]

We can see that the sun represents the Masonic Deity, who is often presented as a **SERPENT** coiled into a circle. On one hand-painted picture of a Masonic apron can be seen numerous Masonic symbols, among them the serpent coiled into a circle, biting its tail. The **SERPENT,** of course, represents **SATAN** and is symbolical of the **SUN!** Osiris is also considered to symbolize the **SUN.** Chapter 2 listed numerous names by which Osiris is known in different nations. One of these names is Sabazius, who is represented with horns and his emblem is a **SERPENT.** He is also considered to be a solar deity (a sun god). With this in mind, it is no surprise to discover that Masonry uses the **SUN** as one of its symbols. It is also amazing to observe the name that the New Agers give to the **SUN.** In the movie, *2010,* by Arthur Clarke,

> ...a new sun suddenly appears radiantly in the sky, bringing peace to earth.... Clarke reveals in his book of the same title just **WHO** this mysterious and peaceful force appearing as the "sun" is: Its name is **LUCIFER.**[34]

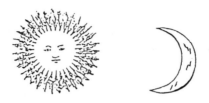

Hutchinson indicates that the "God of Nature [is] symbolized by the **SUN.**"[35] Pan (Satan) is the God of Nature (in mythology), so the **SUN SYMBOLIZES SATAN!** Hutchinson also maintains that "We have retained the Egyptian symbols of the sun and moon...and thereby, we signify, that we are the children of light...."[36] Elsewhere he adds:

> ...we wear the figures of the sun and moon; thence implying, that we...as true Masons, stand redeemed from darkness, and are become the **SONS OF LIGHT....**[37]

Remember, the word **"LUCIFER"** means **"LIGHT BEARER,"** so Masons are the "children of light" or, actually, "the children of **LUCIFER."** Another Masonic writer, Foster Bailey, says:

> Stage by stage They [the Masters of Wisdom] assist at the unfolding of the consciousness of the candidate until the time comes when he can "enter into light," and, in his turn become a **LIGHT-BEARER,** one of the **ILLUMINATI** who can assist the Lodge on High in bringing humanity to light.[38]

The "Masters of Wisdom" are spirit guides (actually **DEMONS**) who are supposedly directing the way to a **ONE WORLD ORDER** and the **ILLUMINATI** is an organization that was founded on May 1, 1776, by Adam Weishaupt.[39] The name "Illuminati" is derived from Lucifer. The Illuminati was dedicated to a **"NEW WORLD ORDER"** or a **"ONE WORLD GOVERNMENT"**—the **EXACT** goal of the **NEW AGERS** today.

The Illuminati plays a part in Masonry, too, for in the listing of "Masonic Chronology" in Waite's book, is this notation: "1776. Foundation of the ILLUMINATI OF BAVARIA, by Adam Weishaupt, on May 1."[40] This date (May 1, 1776) is represented on every dollar bill! If you look at the back of a one dollar bill you will find, on the left-hand side, "MDCCLXXVI" which is 1776 and the words **"NOVUS ORDO SECLORUM"** which means **"NEW WORLD ORDER!"** Des Griffin explains:

> This insignia was adopted by Weishaupt at the time he founded the Order of the Illuminati on May 1, 1776. It is **THAT EVENT** that is memorialized by the "MDCCLXXVI" at the base of the pyramid, and not the date of the signing of the Declaration of Independence, as the uninformed have supposed. It should be noted that this insignia acquired **MASONIC** significance only after the merger of that Order with the Order of the Illuminati....[41]

This left-hand side of the dollar bill also contains a pyramid with the **ALL-SEEING-EYE** above it. You will also notice that the capstone (or cornerstone) has been **REMOVED** and that the **ALL-SEEING-EYE** has **REPLACED** it. Sharon Boyd, writing in the New Age magazine, *What Is,* proclaims:

> Ancient Freemasonry employed the triangle, usually in connection with the **ALL-SEEING EYE.** Throughout the entire system of Masonry, no symbol is more important in its significance—it is the Masonic symbol of the "Grand Architect of the Universe." The entire symbol of the Eye of Providence [the **ALL-SEEING EYE**] in the Radiant Triangle **FORMS A CORNERSTONE OF THE UNFINISHED PYRAMID.**[42]

The Bible specifies that Jesus is the chief **CORNERSTONE,** but He was rejected (Matthew 21:42; I Peter 2:6-7; Psalm 118:22; Mark

12:10; Luke 20:17; Acts 4:11). This is quite evident by looking at the picture—the **CORNERSTONE** has been removed or rejected and has been **REPLACED** by the **ALL-SEEING EYE**—a symbol of Satan! Is it any wonder that the Bible warns us that "the love of money is the root of all evil" (I Timothy 6:10)?

Not only do these symbols actually represent the Masonic god, **LUCIFER,** but there is also **ANOTHER MEANING** behind them. These symbols, as well as others, have **SEXUAL** connotations! For example, let's look at the point within a circle. When a person enters Masonry he is told that the point within a circle represents

>...the individual Mason (the point), contained and restricted by the boundary line of his duty (the circle). Its **REAL MEANING,** however, is that of the phallus, positioned within the female generative principle (sex organ) in sexual union, the climactic act of Sun-worship.[43]

Albert Mackey, a Masonic authority, writes:

>The point within a circle is an interesting and **IMPORTANT** symbol in Freemasonry.... The symbol is really a **BEAUTI-FUL**...allusion to the old **SUN-WORSHIP,** and introduces us for the first time to that modification of it, known among the ancients as the worship of the phallus.[44]

Pike proclaims that Osiris and Isis (who was both his sister **AND** his wife)

>...were commonly symbolized by the generative parts of man and woman...the Phallus and Cteis.... The Indian Lingam was the union of both, as were the boat and mast, and the point within a circle....[45]

He also reminds us that the "**SUN** is still symbolized by the point within a Circle..."[46] and that it is one of "the three Great Lights of the Lodge."[47] What are "the three Great Lights of the Lodge?" These lights are represented as "the Bible, square, and compass."[48]

The compass is the symbol of the Heavens and the square represents the Earth.[49] However, these symbols depict **FAR MORE** than just the heavens and earth. Once again, we find the portrayal of the **PAGAN GODS** in **SYMBOLISM** for Pike mentions that "the heavens and the earth were symbols"[50] for **OSIRIS** and **ISIS**. Also, there is a **SEXUAL** inference. Jim Shaw reports:

> Blue Lodge Masons are taught that the Square is to remind them that they must be "square" in their dealings will all men, i.e. to be honest.... The **REAL MEANING** of these "great lights," however, is **SEXUAL**. The Square represents the female (passive) generative principle, the earth, and the baser sensual nature; and the Compass represents the male (active) generative principle, the sun/heavens, and the higher spiritual nature.[51]

One of the first things a newly initiated Mason does is form a Tau Cross with his feet. While he is blindfolded ("hoodwinked") and before he swears to the Masonic oath, the Mason is made to form "the angle of the oblong square [Tau Cross]"[52] with his feet. The Senior Deacon then shouts **"STAND ERECT!"** even though the person **IS** already erect.[53] Mr. Shaw then expounds to us that this

> ...position of the feet forms the "Tau Cross," a **PHALLIC** symbol from antiquity associated with phallic worship and Sun worship in which the Sun was viewed as the source of life (male), rising each day in the east to impregnate the Earth (female) with new life. Such worship was always done facing the East. Here in the ritual, the command **"STAND ERECT"** is also not a coincidence, and is of obvious symbolic meaning.[54]

The ankh (also called the looped Tau Cross, Crux Ansata, and the Key of the Nile[55]) "was a cross with a coiled **SERPENT** above it...."[56] This "Crux Ansata was the particular emblem of **OSIRIS**...possessing mysterious powers and virtues, as a wonder-working amulet...."[57] Additionally, the

> ...**ANKH** is a symbol of reincarnation and of worship to...the **SUN GOD** of Egypt (**LUCIFER/SATAN**). It also means that in order to worship him in his rites you have given up your virginity and practice orgies.[58]

There are many other Masonic symbols that I won't take the time to analyze, but you can see that **ONE SYMBOL AFTER ANOTHER** has to do with **SATAN** and **SEXUAL** implications! Do not be deceived—Masonry **IS NOT COMPATIBLE** with the Christianity of the Bible, **NO MATTER** what **ANY** Mason tries to tell you.

By now you should be able to realize that Masonry is a worship of **LUCIFER** (through the use of symbols and various gods), but where did it originate? Masonic writers vary quite a bit on this point, but several allege that the origin of Masonry actually goes back to the Garden of Eden. Who was present in Eden? Of course, it was **SATAN**, the **SERPENT!** After the flood, Nimrod, Noah's great-grandson (Genesis 10:8-9) was called "a mighty hunter before the Lord." The word "before" in the Hebrew has several meanings, but one meaning is "against." This is the correct meaning for this word, if you read the entire context. It was Nimrod, you see, who built the tower of Babel in **DEFIANCE** and **REBELLION** against God (Genesis 10:10; 11:2). Masons, however, are **PROUD** of this building for Waite brags:

> As regards Masonry, Babel of course represented a **MASONIC** enterprise and early expositors reaped full benefit from the fact. They remembered that the people who were of "one language and one speech" journeyed from the East towards the West, like those who have tried and proved as Master Masons. When they reached an abiding-place in the land of Shinar, it is affirmed that they dwelt

therein as Noachidae, being the first characteristic name of Masons. It was here that they built their High Tower of Confusion.... Out of evil comes good, however, and (1) the confusion of tongues gave rise to "the antient practice of Masons conversing without the use of speech."[59]

Notice that according to **MASONIC** testimony the evil **WAS NOT** in the building of the tower, but in the confusing of the languages. God confused the languages, so it is implied that God caused the evil, but in spite of this evil, Masons believe, good came because now they converse by means of symbols.

Foster Bailey seems to also look to Babel as a great Masonic enterprise, although he does not mention Babel by name. He states that Masonry "is the descendant of, or is founded upon, a divinely imparted religion...."[60] This religion, he explains,

> ...was the first **UNITED WORLD RELIGION.** Then came the era of separation of many religions, and of sectarianism. Today we are working again towards a **WORLD UNIVERSAL RELIGION.**[61]

Babel fits this description for it was a "unified world religion," but then separation came because God had caused the language to become confused. Of course, Masonry is again working "towards a **WORLD UNIVERSAL RELIGION.**" This is the **EXACT GOAL** of the **NEW AGE MOVEMENT** today, and it was the **EXACT GOAL** of Weishaupt back in the 1700's. In fact, this has been the goal of Satan for 6,000 years! He has wanted a **ONE WORLD RELIGION** and a **ONE WORLD GOVERNMENT** of which **HE** is the head.

Bailey is not the only Mason working towards this goal. Waite admits:

> We know that the world of present values is in the melting-pot and that a **NEW ORDER** is to come.... The purpose of my Masonic life is concerned **SOLELY** with a work in humility **TOWARDS THIS END.**[62]

Benjamin Creme wrote a book through the guidance of a demonic presence[63] in which he states:

> The **NEW RELIGION** will manifest, for instance, through organisations like **MASONRY.** In Freemasonry is embedded the core or the secret heart of the **OCCULT** Mysteries—wrapped up in number, metaphor and symbol....[64]

Bailey asks:

> Is it not possible from a contemplation of this side of Masonic teaching that it may provide **ALL** that is necessary for the formulation of a **UNIVERSAL RELIGION?**[65]

Ralph Anderson gives us this message from the "Tibetan" (a spirit guide or demon who is contacted through meditation) that one of the three main channels that will bring about the **NEW AGE** is **MASONRY!**[66] As a matter of fact, the official journal of Scottish Rite Masonry is called **"THE NEW AGE!"**[67] One prominent Mason brags:

> Now that we are going into the **AGE OF AQUARIUS,** and so many groups are working for the restoration of the mysteries, we Masons are the **PROPER GROUP** to bring these teachings to the world because after all, **THIS IS THE SAME THING WE'VE BEEN TEACHING ALL ALONG.**[68]

Anderson remarks:

> The methods of Deity are demonstrated in its Temples, and under the **ALL-SEEING EYE** the work can go forward. It is a **FAR MORE OCCULT** organisation than can now be realised, and is intended to be the **TRAINING SCHOOL** for the coming **ADVANCED OCCULTISTS.**[69]

One author, who does channeling, points out that those who structured the Masons, Shriners, Moose, and Elks were **CHANNELING** information from **ASCENDED MASTERS (DEMONS).**[70] We are further told by another **OCCULTIST** that Masonry emanates from **SHAMBALLA!**[71] Shamballa is the mythological place where the "Lord of the World," Sanat Kumara (actually Lucifer or Satan), is supposed to live.[72] Constance Cumbey tells us:

> ...Shamballa is what they claim to be the capital city of the Masters of Wisdom and of the whole **SATANIC** hierarchy. They claim it is a city in the Gobi desert.[73]

Alice Bailey, a **NEW AGER,** believes that through group involvement

> ...there can be the inauguration of a new phase of activity in Shamballa. This will enable the Lord of the World to **BECOME THE RULER** of a Sacred Planet which, up to date, has not been the case.[74]

A pamphlet on Shamballa notes: "Our Earth can now become a Sacred Planet, if all right conditions are fulfilled."[75] Bailey reminds us:

From their lofty position in the mystical land of Shamballa the **LEGIONS OF LIGHT** [remember, **LUCIFER MEANS "LIGHT-BEARER!"**]...have announced that time is running out for humanity. They say that our civilization is about to enter a **"NEW AGE"** of enlightenment and that all deserving souls should be ready to take the next step up in cosmic consciousness to a new spiritual understanding.[76]

This brings us to one of the **MAIN GOALS** of the **NEW AGE MOVEMENT** which is a **ONE WORLD GOVERNMENT** with a **ONE WORLD RELIGION,** but for this goal to be realized, a **ONE WORLD LEADER** is needed. Are Masons, like New Agers, also looking for a **ONE WORLD LEADER? YES,** they certainly are! "The true seers have beheld everywhere the same Star in the East [**LUCIFER**] and have come to **ADORE** him who **IS TO BE BORN,"**[77] alleges Waite. Bailey further explains:

The Christ will **REAPPEAR** in physical Presence. Another thing that will happen will be that the ancient Mysteries [**OCCULTISM**] will be restored...those landmarks which **MASONRY** has so earnestly **PRESERVED** and which have been hitherto securely embalmed in the Masonic rituals....

It is these Mysteries which Christ [the Masonic "Christ" or **LUCIFER**] will restore upon His **REAPPEARANCE....**[78]

One of the rituals worked in the ORDER OF LIGHT is called the "Sat B'Hai" which has seven grades which symbolizes the nine incarnations of Vishnu (a Hindu god) with a tenth incarnation **IN THE FUTURE.**[79] This belief is prevalent among the Hindus (and New Agers!). They believe that the god Vishnu has been born time and time again. The first time he was born as a fish, then as a tortoise, then a boar. Finally, he was born as Buddha, but the Hindus are expecting him to be born **ONE MORE TIME IN THE FUTURE.**[80] This time he will be the **SAVIOR OF THE WORLD.** The Hindus call this tenth incarnation **"MAITREYA,"** or the New Age Christ! Waite tells us about this "periodic redeemer." He says: "The tenth incarnation is **STILL TO COME,** being that of a **WARRIOR** on a **MILK-WHITE STEED,** waving over his head the Sword of Destruction...."[81] Another writer describes this tenth incarnation as

...Kalkin, the incarnation **OF THE FUTURE**...a man seated on a **WHITE HORSE** with flaming sword in hand. He will bring judgment to earth and restore the golden age.[82]

These statements are **VERY ASTONISHING** for we are told in Revelation 6 that in the end time four horses will go forth. The first one will be "a **WHITE HORSE:** and he that sat on him had a bow; and a

crown was given unto him: and he went forth conquering, and to conquer" (Revelation 6:2). This is none other than the **ANTICHRIST,** for Christ is **IN HEAVEN** opening the seals. After this **WHITE HORSE** goes forth, war, famine, and death follow. These things would not follow Christ, so this is another indication that the one on the white horse **IS NOT** Christ. So, the **WORLD LEADER** that the New Agers and Masons are looking for is the **ANTICHRIST,** riding upon a **WHITE HORSE!** He will come with great power, performing miracles, and deceiving, if it were possible, even the elect (Mark 13:22). He will also make **WAR** with the saints (Revelation 13:7). Waite even describes this coming leader as a **WARRIOR** with a **SWORD,** and certainly he will fight against those who love God and refuse to follow him. The man of peace that the New Agers are looking for will come in peaceably (Daniel 11:21, 24) but he will not bring **LASTING PEACE.**

After three and one-half years this "man of peace" will break the covenant that he has made with the Jews and will defile their temple. According to Bible prophecy, another Temple **WILL BE** built in Jerusalem but the **ANTICHRIST** will defile it and sit "in the temple of God, shewing himself that he is God" (II Thessalonians 2:4). Concerning the building of this temple, Waite explains that the Zohar teaches that Solomon's Temple

> ...was not built according to the original plans.... In a word, the Lord did not build the House, and they laboured in vain that built it.... **THERE IS A TIME,** however, **TO COME** when the Holy One shall remember His people Israel and the Lord shall build the House.[83]

He continues: "...in the High Grades [of Masonry] we hear of a secret intention to build yet another Temple at Jerusalem."[84] Again we can see that the Masons (whether knowingly or not) are looking, waiting, hoping, and longing for the **ANTICHRIST** and, once again, we see a great **CONFLICT** between Christianity and Masonry.

4. SPIRITUAL SCHIZOPHRENIA

In 1952, Walton Hannah wrote *Darkness Visible*. The purpose of this book was to show that Masonry and Christianity were incompatible. Soon after its publication, an Anglican priest, writing under the pseudonym of Vindex, authored a book entitled *Light Invisible: The Freemason's Answer to Darkness Visible*. This book sought to prove that Masonry and Christianity were compatible and that a person could be a Christian as well as a Mason.[1] The question is, "Are Masonry and Christianity compatible?" Can a person who is a **TRUE BELIEVER** in Jesus Christ and His Word be a Mason?

Vindex alleges:

> As Masons, we believe in God, the Father, Almighty. As Christian Masons we believe in a **SYMBOLICAL** triune essence, and that Jesus Christ is His Son, our Lord.[2]

That quotation **SOUNDS** good and may convince many people that Masonry and Christianity are compatible. However, a closer look at this statement reveals that this is only a belief in a **SYMBOLICAL** trinity. It **IS NOT** a belief in the personal God of the Bible. Vindex continues: "As Moslem Masons we are equally entitled to believe that Mohamet (sic) is His prophet."[3] He then adds a **VERY EN-LIGHTENING** comment:

> With these **SUBSIDIARY [LESSER OR MINOR]** and **SECONDARY** beliefs Masonry **HAS NOTHING TO DO,** giving her members a perfect liberty to interpret the Godhead as they please.[4]

Notice that he calls Christianity a **"SUBSIDIARY AND SECON-DARY"** belief and then plainly informs us that "Masonry **HAS NOTHING TO DO"** with these **INFERIOR** doctrines! So, a Mason, whether he realizes it or not, is relegating his Christian faith to **SECOND PLACE** and putting Masonry first. Matthew 6:24 reminds us: "No man can serve **TWO** masters: for either he will hate the one, and love the other; or else he will hold to the one, and despise the other. Ye **CANNOT** serve God and mammon." Elsewhere Matthew states: "Thou shalt worship the Lord thy God, and Him **ONLY** shalt thou serve" (Matthew 4:10). Remember, Masons have told us that Masonry **IS** a religion.[5] Furthermore, Pike confesses that "Masonry is a **WORSHIP.**"[6]

For Masonry and Christianity to be compatible, **BOTH** must teach **THE SAME BASIC TENETS.** The Bible claims that Jesus Christ is divine (John 1:1-14; 3:13; 5:18; 6:35; 17:3; Philippians 2:6, etc.). What does Masonry tell us about Jesus, the **ONLY** "name under heaven given among men, whereby we must be saved" (Acts 4:12)? Mackey insinuates that the **"REMOVAL** of the name of Jesus and references to Him in Bible verses used in the ritual are **'SLIGHT BUT NECESSARY** modifications.' "[7] Here we are informed that the **REMOVAL** of the precious name of Jesus is **NECESSARY** and it is only a **SLIGHT** modification! For example, *The Masonic Ritualist,* written by Albert Mackey, contains the following charge that is to be read when the Lodge is opened:

> Wherefore, brethren, lay aside all malice, and guile, and hypocrisies, and envies, and all evil speakings.

> If so be ye have tasted that the Lord is gracious, to whom coming as unto a living stone, disallowed indeed of men, but chosen of God, and precious; ye also as living stones, be ye built up a spiritual house, an holy priesthood, to offer up sacrifices acceptable to God....

> (The passages of Scripture here selected are peculiarly appropriate to this degree.... The passages are taken, with **SLIGHT BUT NECESSARY MODIFICATIONS,** from the second chapter of the First Epistle of Peter....)[8]

Would you like to know what **SLIGHT MODIFICATION** was made in this last verse? This verse **ACTUALLY** reads: "Ye also, as lively stones, are built up a spiritual house, an holy priesthood, to offer up spiritual sacrifices, acceptable to God **BY JESUS CHRIST"** (I Peter 2:5). Did you notice that **"BY JESUS CHRIST"** was **DELETED** from the Masonic ritual? Yes, the **REMOVAL** of the name of Jesus Christ from the Lodge is considered to only be a **"SLIGHT BUT NECESSARY MODIFICATION"** to the Mason!

Jim Shaw, a former 33rd degree Mason, knows what happened to him when he mentioned Christ in his prayer. He had been appointed as chaplain and since he did not know how to pray, he contacted a Methodist minister who had joined the Masons. The minister loaned him a book of the prayers of John Wesley. Shaw thought these prayers sounded good so he wrote several of them out. When called on to pray, he read one of Wesley's prayers and ended "in Christ's holy name." Afterwards, he was sharply rebuked and was told that he would be reported. Shortly thereafter he was called on the carpet and warned that he "was **NEVER** to end a prayer 'in Jesus' name' or 'in Christ's name.' " He was commanded to "make [his] prayers **UNIVERSAL.**"[9]

In his informative book, *The Deadly Deception,* Shaw then explains:

> In a "well-ordered Lodge" the name of Jesus is not allowed to be spoken. Praying in His name is a **SERIOUS OFFENSE** and can even bring about the closing of a lodge. When New Testament Scriptures are read in the rituals, portions including the name of Jesus are simply **OMITTED.**[10]

Other Masons have reported the same thing. For example, Harmon Taylor, a former Masonic chaplain, commented: "The **ONLY** instruction I was given as New York State Grand Chaplain, and I was given it **REPEATEDLY,** was not to end a prayer in Jesus' name."[11]

Masons are to make their prayers **UNIVERSAL** and not mention the name of Jesus (so as not to offend Jews or those of other religions), yet Masonry can employ the names of many **PAGAN GODS.** In fact, one book Mackey wrote, entitled *Encyclopedia of Freemasonry,* contains almost 1,000 pages "with articles upon almost every conceivable subject that is in any way related to Freemasonry."[12] Alva McClain adds:

> This Masonic encyclopedia contains articles on almost every false god of the pagan world, but it contains not even a trace of an article on Jesus Christ, the Son of God. This is a significant and ominous omission.[13]

Doesn't the mention of these **PAGAN GODS** offend the Christians? The names of Osiris, Isis, Abaddon, the "God of Nature," etc., can be **FREELY** used, but a Mason can't mention the name of Christ because someone may take offense! Masonry, however, really doesn't care **ONE BIT** about offending the Christian's religion. One quick glance at the ritual for the Shriners (an organization only opened to those Masons who have earned the 32nd degree) clearly illustrates that! The oath for that order states: "...may Allah, the god of Arab, Moslem and Mohammedan, the god our **OUR** fathers, support me...."[14] Not only is Allah mentioned **BY NAME,** but he is called "the god of **OUR** fathers!" This oath, by the way, is sworn on the Koran (the "bible" of the Moslems). The Christian Bible tells us **"SWEAR NOT,** neither by heaven, neither by the earth, neither by any other oath..." (James 5:12). The Bible additionally warns us "make **NO MENTION** of the name of other gods, neither let it be heard out of thy mouth" (Exodus 23:13). It's no wonder that Vindex confesses:

> I, for one, can never understand how **ANYONE** who takes an exclusive view of Christ as the **ONLY** complete revelation of God's truth can become a Freemason without suffering from **SPIRITUAL SCHIZOPHRENIA**.[15]

In other words, Vindex states that he cannot see how someone who **TRULY BELIEVES** what the Bible says about Jesus being the **ONLY** name given under heaven by which humankind can be saved (see Acts 4:12), can be a Mason. This statement, let me remind you, comes from a **MASON** who wrote a book trying to show the **COMPATIBILITY** between Masonry and Christianity!

Another area that can cause "spiritual schizophrenia" is the Masonic belief in the resurrection. You may ask, "Don't Christians believe in the resurrection?" Yes, we do, but we don't believe in the resurrection taught by Masonry. Waite stresses that a belief in the resurrection is necessary before one can join the Masons.[16] Of course, he quickly explains what is meant by "resurrection."

> Belief in God and in resurrection to a future life—the latter **NOT** connoting **PHYSICAL RESURRECTION**—are conditions in the absence of which no person can be made a Mason.[17]

He also remarks:

> The passage of the soul from a sacramental death into a mystical and immortal life is the subject of all those old Mysteries which know nothing of **MATERIAL** [or **BODILY**] resurrection.[18]

So, when Masons speak of a resurrection they **DO NOT** mean a **LITERAL, PHYSICAL** resurrection of the dead as the Bible teaches (see I Corinthians 15:1-58), but rather **REINCARNATION.**

There is ample Masonic testimony dealing with the belief in reincarnation. Wilmshurst refers to reincarnation in his writings, but since he felt some of his readers would not accept the idea, he said he wouldn't press the issue too far.[19] Albert Mackey embraced the belief in reincarnation.[20] In fact, the 31st degree in Masonry deals with the theory of reincarnation. Jim Shaw expounds:

> In this degree the candidate, as a typical man who has just died, is defending his life before the **GODS AND GODDESSES** of Egypt. The candidate tells of his good works in his just-ended life and of his hope for a better incarnation in the next. As the candidate

tells of each work he has done, one of the Egyptian deities drops a stone into a pan of a scale. As the last stone is dropped into the pan by the god Anubis (a man with a ram's head), the scale tips and Osiris and Isis, who are presiding, say, "Weighed in the balance and found wanting." The candidate listens then as the Soul of Cheres, symbol of immortality, is brought before the Chamber of the Dead and he learns that he must improve in his **NEXT LIFE** in order to advance in the cycle of **REINCARNATION.**[21]

By now you should realize that there is a direct **CONFLICT** between Masonry and Christianity, but you may ask, "Aren't the Masons good, moral-living people and don't they teach Biblical principles like honesty?" That's a good question. Waite answers that Masonry "is **ON THE SURFACE** a 'system of morality, veiled in allegory and illustrated by symbols.' "[22] Do you **HONESTLY** feel that **ANY** organization that perpetrates **LIES AND DECEIT** is to be considered as a **MORAL** group? Masonry **INTENTIONALLY** lies **OVER AND OVER** again and again to the newly initiated Mason and only gradually reveals the **TRUE** nature of its **DIABOLICAL** purposes. Masonry tells the newcomer that the symbolism of the square represents that he should be "square" in his dealings[23] never disclosing to the candidate that the **REAL MEANING** is **SEXUAL.** Masonry claims there is **NO CONFLICT** between itself and Christianity[24] never telling the truth about the "necessary" **DELE- TION** of the precious name of Jesus Christ. Masonry teaches the new Mason that the "G" in the Lodge stands for "God" and later on he is told that it represents "Geometry"[25] but it refuses to admit to the **NEWCOMER** who the **TRUE GOD** of Masonry is. Do you consider these **ADMIRABLE** traits?

Masonry does not only lie to its fellow companions, but it instructs the individual Masons to **LIE** to their families! They **MUST** lie to safeguard the secrets. For example, Masons are notified:

If your wife, or child, or friend, should ask you anything about your initiation—as for instance, if your clothes were taken off, if you were blindfolded, if you had a rope around your neck, etc, you **MUST** conceal....hence of course, you must **DELIBERATELY LIE** about it. It is part of your obligation.[26]

As Masons climb the Masonic ladder their oaths contain instructions not to testify against a brother Mason even though he has committed a crime. The Mason, taking the oath of the 3rd degree, promises to conceal all crimes committed by a fellow Mason **EXCEPT** those of treason and murder.[27] However, by the 13th degree, the oath is taken to the effect that **ALL CRIMES** are to be covered and concealed, **EVEN** murder and treason.[28] This means that if a Mason has committed murder and the judge is also a Mason, the judge is **OBLIGATED** by his Masonic oath to set the murderer free. This may even mean placing the blame on an **INNOCENT** person! In fact, this command is given in one handbook:

You **MUST CONCEAL ALL** the crimes of your brother Masons...and should you be summoned as a witness against a brother Mason be always sure to shield him.... **IT MAY BE PERJURY** to do this, it is true, but you're keeping your obligations.[29]

Masons are actually taught to lie but the Bible forbids it. God's Word specifies: "Lie not one to another..." (Colossians 3:9). Proverbs 6:16-17 cautions us that there are seven things that God hates and one of them is "a lying tongue." Of course, you can expect Masons to lie because the **TRUE GOD** of Masonry is **LUCIFER** and John 8:44 tells us that he "is a liar, and the father of it."

Masonry not only **IS NOT** a moral organization, it is also **VERY SELECTIVE** about those who can join. Masonry claims to be the way to gain entrance into the Celestial Lodge above, yet many people are denied admission to the Masonic Lodge. Anderson mentions that

"Freemasonry is available to **ANY** man of good character who believes in a Supreme Being.... There are **NO RESTRICTIONS** relating to race, creed, or color."[30] This is just another Masonic lie. Actually, no women, children, lame, blind, deaf, retarded, slaves, or Negroes are allowed to join the Masons. Waite informs us: "Whoever is capable of election to the Kingdom of Heaven is a fit and proper person to be made a Mason."[31] That **SOUNDS** good, but there just happens to be a catch. Notice that he states: "Whoever is **CAPABLE** of election to the Kingdom of Heaven...." He then goes on to advise us who **IS NOT** capable of the Kingdom of Heaven. Masonry

...does not open them to **MINORS** because their time is not yet, nor to the mens insana because that—qua mens insana—is not capable of election to the Kingdom of Heaven....[32]

This, of course, excludes children and the insane. Hutchinson tells us that "it is necessary that a candidate for Masonry should be able to declare that he is the son of a free woman."[33] This excludes the slaves. Wilmshurst declares: "The true candidate must indeed needs be...a 'white man'...."[34] "American blacks have been, in general, excluded from Masonic membership."[35] However, there is a group of Negro Masons known as Prince Hall Masonry,[36] but Jim Shaw remarks:

There is a Negro Masonic system, called the Prince Hall Lodge, but **IT IS NOT ASSOCIATED IN ANY WAY** with "white" Freemasonry. It is referred to as "clandestine" Masonry, and it is considered by the rest of Masonry to be a spurious, illegitimate imitation.[37]

The Lodge excludes and rejects the blind, for they cannot see to engage in the signs and due-guards; it rejects the crippled and maimed, for they cannot assume the body positions necessary for the signs and due-guards. The deaf are excluded because they cannot hear the "secret" words. The poor are excluded, for they cannot pay the fees and dues. The feeble-minded are rejected because they cannot learn and function in the Lodge. The emotionally ill are rejected because they cannot be trusted with the "secrets."[38]

Even though Masonry is supposed to lead to the admission into the Celestial Lodge above, so many are **FORBIDDEN** entrance into its organization. These "rejects" of Masonry are **WELCOMED** by Jesus Christ. Both slave and free are invited to come to Christ for "by one Spirit are we all baptized into one body, whether we be Jews or Gentiles, whether we be bond or free..." (I Corinthians 12:13). "Knowing that whatsoever good thing any man doeth, the same shall he receive of the Lord, whether he be bond or free" (Ephesians 6:8). Children were encouraged to come to Christ and He said "Suffer [allow or permit] little children, and forbid them not, to come unto Me: **FOR OF SUCH IS THE KINGDOM OF HEAVEN**" (Matthew 19:14). Waite contends that the kingdom of heaven is not opened "to minors because their time is not yet"[39] but "Jesus called a little child unto Him.... And said...**EXCEPT** ye be converted, and become as little children, ye shall not enter into the kingdom of heaven" (Matthew 18:2-3).

The poor could come and receive the same gift of eternal life as the rich could. James, a brother to Jesus, gives us an illustration along this line. He said that if a well-dressed, wealthy person and a poorly-clad, poor person would enter a group and if the rich person were given the preeminence and the poor person ignored or relegated to a lowly position, that that would be sin. "If ye have respect to persons, ye commit sin..." (James 2:2-3, 9). Yet the poor are **EXCLUDED** from Masonic Lodges because they cannot afford to pay the entrance fee.

The outcasts of society, such as the lepers, were healed and received by Christ. The lame, blind, deaf, sick, and even demon possessed, could all be healed by Christ's touch. He even reminds us that "they that be whole need not a physician, but they that are sick... for I am not come to call the righteous, but sinners to repentance" (Matthew 9:12-13). "Come unto Me, **ALL** ye that labour and are heavy laden, and I will give you rest" (Matthew 11:28). **"WHOSOEVER WILL,** let him take the water of life **FREELY"** (Revelation 22:17b). **ALL** are invited to come to Christ and there is **NO CHARGE**—it's a **FREE** gift. Christ paid the price by dying on the cross for your sins and mine. All we have to do is **ACCEPT** the gift. Jesus said: "Him that cometh to Me I will **IN NO**

WISE cast out" (John 6:37b). Yes, Jesus accepts those that Masonry rejects. Once again we find that Masonry and Christianity are **INCOMPATIBLE.** Even Albert Mackey admits that "the **RELIGION** of Freemasonry...**IS NOT** Christianity."[40] *Chase's Digest of Masonic Law* informs us:

> In fact Blue Lodge Masonry [the first three degrees of Masonry] **HAS NOTHING WHATEVER TO DO WITH THE BIBLE.** It **IS NOT** founded on the Bible; if it was (sic) it would not be Masonry; it would be something else.[41]

If you are a Mason who is also interested in following Christ, you have a decision to make. **EITHER** you can continue on in Masonry and pay homage and worship to **LUCIFER OR** you must renounce your membership and follow Christ. "Be ye not **UNEQUALLY** yoked together with unbelievers: for what fellowship hath righteousness with unrighteousness? and what communion hath light with darkness? And what concord hath Christ with Belial? or what part hath he that believeth with an infidel? And what agreement hath the temple of God with idols?...Wherefore **COME OUT FROM AMONG THEM** and **BE YE SEPARATE,** saith the Lord, and **TOUCH NOT** the unclean thing; and I will receive you..." (II Corinthians 6:14-17). "No man can serve **TWO** masters: for either he will hate the one, and love the other; or else he will hold to the one, and despise the other. Ye **CANNOT** serve God and mammon" (Matthew 6:24). "Thou shalt worship the Lord thy God, and Him **ONLY** shalt thou serve" (Matthew 4:10). "Have **NO FELLOWSHIP** with the unfruitful works of darkness, but rather **REPROVE** them" (Ephesians 5:11).

To those who have not yet joined Masonry but are leaning that way, consider the consequences. Are you willing to pledge your allegiance to **LUCIFER?** Are you willing to partake in **PAGAN AND OCCULTIC** ceremonies with **SEXUAL** overtones? Do you feel comfortable taking an oath to protect fellow Masons who may have committed murder or other crimes? These are just a few of the items that need to be considered.

If you have never accepted Christ as your **PERSONAL** Savior and you would like to do so, the first step is to be born again. John 3:3: "**EXCEPT** a man be born **AGAIN,** he **CANNOT** see the kingdom of God." How can one be born **AGAIN?** We all know that we were born once, our physical birth, but can we enter into our mother's womb and be born the second time (see John 3:1-17)? No. The second birth comes by being born into the family of God. John 3:16: "For God so

LOVED the world [that includes **YOU!**] that He **GAVE** His only Begotten Son, that **WHOSOEVER** [that includes **YOU**] **BE-LIEVETH** [trusts, clings to, relies on] Him [God's Son, Jesus] should not perish [in hell], but have everlasting life." All you need to do is sincerely believe with all your heart that Jesus is the Son of God and to be willing to turn from your sins and ask Jesus to come into your heart and help you to live for Him, and He **WILL** do it. John 6:37: "Him that cometh to Me I will **IN NO WISE** cast out." I John 1:9: "If we **CONFESS** our sins [not to men, but to God], He is **FAITHFUL** and **JUST** to **FORGIVE** us our sins, and to **CLEANSE** us from **ALL** unrighteousness." Romans 10:9: "If thou shalt **CONFESS** with thy mouth the Lord Jesus, and shalt **BELIEVE** in thine heart that God hath raised Him from the dead, thou **SHALT** be saved [born again]."

If you would like to be born again, pray your own prayer or sincerely pray the following: *Dear Jesus, I realize that I am a sinner. I believe that You died for my sins. Please forgive me of my past sins and come into my heart. Save me for Your sake, and help me to live for You. I ask this in Your name. Amen.*

If you sincerely prayed and asked Jesus to forgive you of your sins, you will have the assurance that you are now a child of God. John 1:12: "But **AS MANY** as received Him, to them gave He power to become the sons of God, even to them that **BELIEVE** on His name." "Therefore if any man be in Christ, he is a new creature: old things are passed away; behold all things are become new" (II Corinthians 5:17). Read your Bible **EVERY** day (start with the book of John), and find a Bible-believing church where you can worship God with other born again believers.

ENDNOTES

CHAPTER 1: IS FREE MASONRY FREE?

1 W. L. Wilmshurst, *The Meaning of Masonry* (Bell Publishing Company, reprint of fifth edition published in 1927), p. 19.

2 Delmar Duane Darrah, *History and Evolution of Freemasonry* (Chicago, Illinois: Charles T. Powner Company, 1954), p. 335.

3 *Ibid.,* p. 337.

4 Richard DeHaan, "Fraternal Organizations," *Collier's Encyclopedia,* 1978 ed., Vol. 10, p. 341.

5 Albert Pike, *Morals and Dogma of the Ancient and Accepted Scottish Rite of Freemasonry* (Richmond, Virginia: L. H. Jenkins, Inc., 1919), p. 384.

6 *Ibid.*

7 Ralph Anderson, "Freemasonry: Yesterday, Today and Tomorrow," *Arcana Workshops* (June 1985), p. 5.

8 Arthur Edward Waite, *A New Encyclopedia of Freemasonry and of Cognate Instituted Mysteries: Their Rites, Literature and History* (New York: Weathervane Books, 1970), Vol. II, p. 421.

9 *Arcana Workshops, op. cit.,* pp. 3-4. See also Foster Bailey, *The Spirit of Masonry,* (Kent, England: Lucis Press Limited, 1957), pp. 28-29.

10 Waite, *op. cit.,* p. 395.

11 Pike, *op. cit.,* p. 148.

12 *Ibid.,* p. 106.

13 *Ibid.,* p. 105.

14 *Ibid.,* p. 819.

15 *Ibid.,* pp. 104-105.

16 *Arcana Workshops, op. cit.,* p. 2.

17 Dave Hunt, *The Cult Explosion: An Expose of Today's Cults and Why They Prosper* (Eugene, Oregon: Harvest House Publishers, 1980), p. 78.

18 Alva McClain, *Freemasonry and Christianity* (Winona Lake, Indiana: BMH Books, 1980 edition), pp. 9-10.

19 *Arcana Workshops, op. cit.,* p. 3.

20 Pike, *op. cit.,* p. 213.

21 Waite, *op. cit.,* p. 479.

22 Pike, *op. cit.,* p. 219.

23 *Ibid.,* p. 11. See also *Collier's Encyclopedia, op. cit.,* p. 340.

24 Waite, *op. cit.,* p. 433.

25 Charles E. Green, *History of the Grand Lodge of A. F. and A. M. of Delaware,* (n. p., 1956), p. 228.

26 Darrah, *op. cit.,* p. 298.

27 *Collier's Encyclopedia, op. cit.,* p. 341.

28 Jim Shaw and Tom McKenney, *The Deadly Deception: Freemasonry Exposed. . .By One of Its Top Leaders* (Lafayette, Louisiana: Huntington House, Inc.), p. 26

29 Wilmshurst, *op. cit.,* p. 35.

30 *Ibid.*

31 *Ibid.*

32 Waite, *op. cit.,* Vol. I, p. 395.

33 *Ibid.*

34 Wilmshurst, *op. cit.,* p. 39.

35 *Ibid.,* p. 40.

36 *Ibid.,* pp. 100-101.

37 William Hutchinson, *The Spirit of Masonry,* revised by Rev. George Oliver, originally published in 1775 (New York: Bell Publishing Company, 1982), p. 310.

38 Waite, *op. cit.,* pp. 55-56.

39 Wilmshurst, *op. cit.,* p. 146.

40 *Ibid.,* p. 46.

41 *Ibid.,* p. 163.

42 *Arcana Workshops, op. cit.*

43 Waite, *op. cit.,* p. 421.

44 Wilmshurst, *op. cit.,* p. 51.

45 Waite, *op. cit.,* p. 314.

46 Foster Bailey, *The Spirit of Masonry,* (Kent, England: Lucis Press Limited, 1957), p. 113.

47 Wilmshurst, *op. cit.,* p. 92.

48 *Ibid.,* p. 62.

49 *Ibid.,* p. 93.

50 Waite, *op. cit.,* p. 100.

51 Pike, *op. cit.,* p. 592.

52 Waite, *op. cit.,* Vol. I, p. ix.

53 Pike, *op. cit.,* p. 202.

54 Harry E. Wedeck, *The Treasury of Witchcraft* (New York: Philosophical Library, 1961), caption under picture between pp. 170-171.

55 "Complete Occult Digest A to Z," 1984 catalog from International Imports, p. 104.

56 Wilmshurst, *op. cit.,* p. 94.

57 Darrah, *op. cit.,* p. 279.

58 Shaw and McKenney, *op. cit.,* p. 130.

59 Wilmshurst, *op. cit.*

60 *Ibid.,* p. 33.

61 Waite, *op. cit.,* Vol. II, p. 409.

62 *Ibid.,* Vol. I, p. x.

63 Hutchinson, *op. cit.,* pp. 180-181. See also Waite, *Ibid.*

64 *Ibid.,* pp. 332-333.

65 Waite, *op. cit.,* p. 443.

66 J. Edward Decker, Jr., *The Question of Freemasonry* (Issaquah, Washington: Free the Masons Ministries, n. d.), pp. 10-11.

67 C. J. S. Thompson, *The Mysteries and Secrets of Magic* (New York, New York: Causeway Books, 1973), p. 112.

2 WHO IS THE GOD OF MASONRY?

1   *Arcana Workshops, op. cit.,* p. 2.

2   C. Penney Hunt, *Masons and Christ: The Menace of Freemasonry* (Finleyville, Pennsylvania: The Voice of the Nazarene Press, 1967), p. 9.

3   Paul Hamlyn, *Greek Mythology* (London, England: Paul Hamlyn Limited, 1967), pp. 109, 114.

4   *Ibid.,* p. 113.

5   *Ibid.*

6   *Ibid.,* p. 112.

7   Shaw and McKenney, *op. cit.,* pp. 150-151.

8   *Ibid.,* p. 153.

9   Geoffrey Parrinder, ed., *World Religions from Ancient History to the Present* (New York, New York: Facts on File Publications, 1971), p. 176. See also "Osiris," *The World Book Encyclopedia,* 1961 ed., Vol. 13, p. 654.

10 Waite, *op. cit.,* Vol. II, p. 169.

11 *Collier's Encyclopedia, op. cit.,* p. 338.

12 Wilmshurst, *op. cit.,* p. 142.

13 "Isis," *Encyclopaedia Britannica,* 1964 ed., Vol. 12, p. 703.

14 *Ibid.*

15 Pike, *op. cit.,* pp. 15, 377, 401, 405, 504, etc.

16 Waite, *op. cit.,* Vol. I, pp. 342-343.

17 Darrah, *op. cit.,* p. 298.

18 Waite, *op. cit.,* p. 440.

19 Wilmshurst, *op. cit.,* p. 31.

20 Waite, *op. cit.,* Vol. II, p. 38.

21 Wilmshurst, *op cit.,* p. 136.

22 *Ibid.*

23 *Ibid.* See also Pike, *op. cit.,* p. 496.

24 Pike, *op. cit.,* p. 407.

25 *Ibid.*

26 Hutchinson, *op. cit.,* p. 82.

27 *Ibid.,* pp. 82-83.

28 Pike, *op. cit.*

29 Dave Hunt and Ed Decker, *The God Makers: A Shocking Expose of What the Mormon Church Really Believes* (Eugene, Oregon: Harvest House Publishers, 1984), p. 197.

30 Bob Larson, *Larson's Book of Cults* (Wheaton, Illinois: Tyndale House Publishers, Inc., 1982), p. 75.

31 Shaw and McKenney, *op. cit.,* p. 102.

32 Pike, *op. cit.,* p. 495.

33 *Ibid.*

34 *Ibid.*

35 *Ibid.,* pp. 499-500.

36 *Ibid.,* p. 502.

37 *Ibid.,* p. 368.

38 "Bel," *Encyclopaedia Britannica,* 1964 ed., Vol. 3, p. 410.

39 Texe Marrs, *Mystery Mark of the New Age: Satan's Design for World Domination* (Westchester, Illinois: Crossway Books, 1988), p. 91.

40 Stephen Knight, *The Brotherhood: The Secret World of the Freemasons* (Briarcliff Manor, New York: Stein and Day, 1984), p. 236.

41 *Ibid.*

42 Pike, *op. cit.*

43 Einar Haugen, "Thor," *The World Book Encyclopedia,* 1961 ed., Vol. 17, p. 204.

44 *Ibid.*

45 Max Wood, *Rock and Roll: An Analysis of the Music* (n. p., n. d.), p. 28.

46 *Ibid.,* p. 30.

47 *Ibid.,* p. 31.

48 Hutchinson, *op. cit.,* pp. 47-48.

49 *Ibid.,* p. 48.

50 *Ibid.,* p. 85.

51 Pike, *op. cit.,* p. 321. See also A. Ralph Epperson, *The Unseen Hand: An Introduction to the Conspiratorial View of History* (Tucson, Arizona: Publius Press, 1985), p. 224.

52 Waite, *op. cit.,* Vol. I, p. 424.

53 *Ibid.,* Vol. II, p. 468.

54 *Ibid.,* p. 415.

55 Hutchinson, *op. cit.,* p. 80.

56 Wilmshurst, *op. cit.,* p. 127.

57 Waite, *op. cit.,* Vol. I, p. ix.

58 "Mithras," *The World Book Encyclopedia,* 1961 ed., Vol. 12, p. 566.

59 *Ibid.*

60 Shaw and McKenney, *op. cit.,* p. 156.

61 *Ibid.*

62 *Ibid.,* p. 157.

63 Constance Cumbey, *The Hidden Dangers of the Rainbow: The New Age Movement and Our Coming Age of Barbarism* (Shreveport, Louisiana: Huntington House, Inc., 1983), p. 136.

64 Decker, *op. cit.,* p. 6.

65 Waite, *op. cit.,* Vol. II, p. 253.

66 *Ibid., p. 278.*

67 Shaw and McKenney, *op. cit.,* p. 62.

68 Texe Marrs, "Masons Are a Secret New Age Cult," *Flashpoint* (March 1990), p. 3.

69 Hutchinson, *op. cit.,* pp. 101, 209.

70 Waite, *op. cit.,* p. 470.

71 Wilmshurst, *op. cit.,* p. 136.

72 Knight, *op. cit.,* p. 236.

73 *Ibid.*

74 *Ibid.*

75 C. Penney Hunt, *op. cit.,* p. 18.

76 *Ibid.*
77 Waite, *op. cit.,* p. 405.
78 "Bel," *The World Book Encyclopedia,* 1961 ed., Vol. 2, p. 173.
79 "Pan," *The World Book Encyclopedia,* 1961 ed., Vol. 14, p. 93.
80 *Ibid.*
81 International Imports, *op. cit.,* p. 115.
82 Hutchinson, *op. cit.,* p. 62.
83 *Ibid.,* p. 115.
84 Wilmshurst, *op. cit.,* pp. 209-210.

3. SYMBOLS OF MASONRY

1   Waite, *op. cit.,* p. 108.
2   Sybil Leek, *Numerology: The Magic of Numbers* (New York, New York: The MacMillian Company, 1969), p. 124.
3   Wedeck, *op. cit.,* p. 59.
4   International Imports, *op. cit.,* p. 252.
5   *Ibid.,* p. 117.
6   *Ibid.*
7   Marrs, *Mystery Mark of the New Age, op. cit.,* p. 95. See also Rudolf Koch, *The Book of Signs* (New York, New York: Dover Publications, Inc., 1955 ed.), p. 6.
8   *Ibid.,* p. 97.
9   Gary Jennings, *Black Magic, White Magic* (Eau Claire, Wisconsin: The Dial Press, Inc., 1964), p. 51.
10 Wood, *op. cit.*
11 "Freemasonry," *Encyclopaedia Britannica,* 1964 ed., Vol. 9, p. 844.
12 Thompson, *op. cit.,* p. 178.
13 *Self-Help Update* (1985), Issue 26, p. 13.
14 *Ibid.,* p. 12.
15 Hutchinson, *op. cit.,* p. 195.
16 *Ibid.,* p. 111.
17 *Ibid.*
18 *Ibid.,* p. 209.
19 Decker, *op. cit.*
20 Pike, *op. cit.,* pp. 104-105.
21 International Imports, *op. cit.,* p. 100.
22 Decker, *op. cit.,* p. 12.
23 Waite, *op. cit.,* p. 109.
24 Pike, *op. cit.,* p. 506.
25 Waite, *op. cit.,* p. 108.
26 Pike, *op. cit.,* p. 16.
27 *Ibid.,* p. 477.
28 Alice A. Bailey, *Discipleship in the New Age* (New York: Lucis Publishing Company, 1955), Vol. II, pp. 262, 265.
29 Jennings, *op. cit.,* p. 49.

30   *Ibid.*

31   Jack T. Chick, *Spellbound* (Chino, California: Chick Publications, 1978), p. 7.

32   Waite, *op. cit.,* p. 110.

33   Jennings, *op. cit.,* p. 47.

34   Marrs, *Mystery Mark of the New Age, op. cit.,* pp. 90-91.

35   Hutchinson, *op. cit.,* p. 93.

36   *Ibid.,* p. 209.

37   *Ibid.,* p. 278.

38   Foster Bailey, *op. cit.,* p. 23.

39   A. Ralph Epperson, *The Unseen Hand: An Introduction to the Conspiratorial View of History* (Tucson, Arizona: Publius Press, 1985), p. 78.

40   Waite, *op. cit.,* p. 67.

41   Des Griffin, *The Fourth Reich of the Rich* (Emissary Publications, 1978), p. 95.

42   Sharon Boyd, "Occult America: The U. S. Founded on Occultism, Not Christianity," *What Is,* Vol. 1, No. 2, p. 13.

43   Shaw and McKenney, *op. cit.,* p. 144.

44   *Ibid.,* p. 145.

45   Pike, *op. cit.,* p. 401.

46   *Ibid.,* p. 486.

47   *Ibid.*

48   Shaw and McKenney, *op. cit.,* p. 27.

49   Pike, *op. cit.,* p. 851.

50   *Ibid.,* p. 401.

51   Shaw and McKenney, *op. cit.,* p. 143.

52   *Ibid.,* p. 25.

53   *Ibid.*

54   *Ibid.,* p. 29.

55   Rudolf Koch, *The Book of Signs* (New York, New York: Dover Publications, Inc., 1955), p. 19.

56   Pike, *op. cit.,* p. 502.

57   *Ibid.,* p. 504.

58   Chick, *op. cit.*

59   Waite, *op. cit.,* Vol. I, pp. 61-62.

60   Foster Bailey, *op. cit.,* p. 31.

61   *Ibid.*

62   Waite, *op. cit.,* p. 175.

63   Benjamin Creme, *The Reappearance of the Christ and the Masters of Wisdom* (North Hollywood, California: Tara Center, 1980), p. 5.

64   *Ibid.,* p. 87.

65   Foster Bailey, *op. cit.,* p. 113.

66   *Arcana Workshops, op. cit.,* p. 5.

67   Waite, *op. cit.,* p. 76.

68   *The New Age Movement—Age of Aquarius—Age of Antichrist,* An Interview with Constance Cumbey (Oklahoma City, Oklahoma: The Southwest Radio Church, 1982), pp. 27-28.

69 *Arcana Workshops, op. cit.,* pp. 5-6.

70 Carla A. Rueckert, *A Channeling Handbook* (Louisville, Kentucky: L/L Research, 1987), p. 3.

71 Alice A. Bailey, *Discipleship in the New Age* (New York: Lucis Publishing Company, 1972), Vol. I, p. 171.

72 Creme, *op. cit.,* p. 73.

73 *Is the Antichrist in the World Today?,* An Interview with Constance Cumbey (Oklahoma City, Oklahoma: The Southwest Radio Church, 1982), pp. 27-28.

74 Alice Bailey, *Discipleship, op. cit.,* Vol. II, p. 326.

75 Shamballa: Where the Will of God Is Known (New York, New York: Arcane School, n. d.), p. 27.

76 Alice Bailey, *Discipleship, op. cit.,* Vol. I, p. 439.

77 Waite, *op. cit.,* Vol. II, p. 416.

78 Alice A. Bailey, *The Reappearance of the Christ* (Lucis Publishing Company, 1948), pp. 121-122.

79 Waite, *op. cit.,* p. 406.

80 *Ibid.* See also Parrinder, *op. cit.,* p. 223.

81 *Ibid.*

82 Parrinder, *op. cit.*

83 Waite, *op. cit.,* pp. 486-487.

84 *Ibid.,* p. 487.

4. SPIRITUAL SCHIZOPHRENIA

1 Knight, *op. cit.,* pp. 232-233.

2 *Ibid.,* p. 233.

3 *Ibid.*

4 *Ibid.*

5 *Arcana Workshops, op. cit.,* p. 3.; Dave Hunt, *op. cit.*; Pike, *op. cit.,* p. 213.; Waite, *op. cit.,* p. 479.

6 Pike, *op. cit.,* p. 219.

7 Shaw and McKenney, *op. cit.,* p. 129. See also McClain, *op. cit.,* p. 23.

8 McClain, *op. cit.,* pp. 22-23.

9 Shaw and McKenney, *op. cit.,* p. 72.

10 *Ibid.,* pp. 29-30.

11 *Ibid.,* p. 136.

12 McClain, *op. cit.,* p. 7.

13 *Ibid.,* p. 19.

14 Shaw and McKenney, *op. cit.,* p. 139. See also Decker, *op. cit.,* p. 8.

15 Knight, *op. cit.,* p. 234.

16 Waite, *op. cit.,* p. 310. See also *Collier's Encyclopedia, op. cit.,* p. 340.

17 *Ibid.*

18 *Ibid.,* p. 334.

19 Wilmshurst, *op. cit.,* p. 195.

20 Shaw and McKenney, *op. cit.,* p. 84.

21 *Ibid.,* p. 85.

22 Waite, *op. cit.,* p. 421.

23 Shaw and McKenney, *op. cit.,* p. 143.

24 Darrah, *op. cit.*

25 Hutchinson, *op. cit.,* p. 148.

26 Shaw and McKenney, *op. cit.,* p. 137.

27 *Ibid.* See also Knight, *op. cit.*

28 *Ibid.*

29 *Ibid.*

30 *Arcana Workshops, op. cit.,* p. 2.

31 Waite, *op. cit.,* p. 309.

32 *Ibid.,* p. 310.

33 Hutchinson, *op. cit.,* p. 34.

34 Wilmshurst, *op. cit.,* p. 12.

35 *Collier's Encyclopedia, op. cit.*

36 See Joseph A. Walkes, Jr., *Jno. G. Lewis, Jr.—End of an Era: The History of the Prince Hall Grand Lodge of Louisiana 1842-1979* (n. p., 1986).

37 Shaw and McKenney, *op. cit.,* p. 29.

38 *Ibid.,* p. 147. NOTE: Although it has been the normal practice of Masonry not to accept the handicapped and black, some lodges have now relaxed their guidelines and allow the blind, lame, and blacks to join.

39 Waite, *op. cit.*

40 Dave Hunt, *op. cit.,* p. 78. See also McClain, *op. cit.,* p. 11.

41 Shaw and McKenney, *op. cit.,* p. 129.

OTHER LITERATURE BY CATHY BURNS

BOOK:

Alcoholics Anonymous Unmasked (126 pages)

BOOKLETS:

Eternal Life

Questions and Answers About the New Age Movement

To Catholics with Love

What Is Your I.Q.?

ARTICLES:

Astrology and Your Future

Chart Your Course with Orion International

Divination

Divorce and Remarriage

Dowsing Is in the Bible!

Hidden Dangers of Reflexology

Hypnosis: Cure or Curse?

I Have Sinned

Jason Winters and His Herbal Tea

Miscegenation

Mormonism (3 part series)

    1. Mormonism and Its History

    2. Some Doctrines of Mormonism

    3. Mormonism and Godhood

New Age Love

Some Occult Terms Explained

Speaking in Tongues and Related Issues (14 part series)

    1. Do All Speak in Tongues?

    2. Baptism in the Holy Ghost

    3. Sinful Lives and Tongues

    4. Signs and Wonders

TRACTS:

For a price list and other literature that is available,
write to:

SHARING
212-M E. 7th St.
Mt. Carmel, PA. 17851-2211